BEHIND PRISON WALLS

LISTING OF PREVIOUS BOOKS
BY CORVALIS HODGES

* * *

TOUCHED BY AN ANGEL:

A Spiritual Motivational Book

JEHOVAH SERMONETTES:

An Empowering Uplifting Daily Bread

RISING ABOVE YOUR STRUGGLES:

Life-transforming Truth

BEHIND PRISON WALLS

Inmate Number 27773-016

Behind Prison Walls

Inmate Number 27772-016

Corvalis G. Hodges

Copyright © 2009 by Corvalis G. Hodges.

Library of Congress Control Number:		2009902449
ISBN:	Hardcover	978-1-4415-1096-9
	Softcover	978-1-4415-1095-2

All rights reserved. No part of this book may be reproduced in any form, except by a newspaper, magazine, or book reviewer who wishes to quote verbatim brief passages in connection with a review.

Editorial, sales and distribution, rights, and permissions inquiries should be addressed to the author and publisher in writing at

To keep in line with the integrity of the author's voice, grammar and, in some cases, spelling has not been altered/edited.

All scriptures in this book are from the Holy Bible, New King James Version.

This book was printed in the United States of America.

To order additional copies of this book, contact:
Xlibris Corporation
1-888-795-4274
www.Xlibris.com
Orders@Xlibris.com
59027

CONTENTS

Acknowledgment of Gratitude 7
Dedication 9
Special Dedication to Women 11
What Others Are Saying 15
Introduction 19

PART ONE

FPC Alderson Program 21

PART TWO

Chapter 1 45
Chapter 2 47
Chapter 3 49
Chapter 4 51
Chapter 5 54
Chapter 6 56
Chapter 7 62
Chapter 8 64
Chapter 9 66
Chapter 10 68
Chapter 11 70
Chapter 12 72
Chapter 13 74

PART THREE

God Will Make a Loser Win 79
Treatment 80
Letting Go and Letting God 81
God, You Have Failed Me 82

To My Sister with Love 84
Stopping the Generational Curse Cycle 85
When Our Dreams Are Shattered 88
Stones Can't Stop Us 94
Living In Troublesome Times 100
The Riches of God's Grace 104
Real Commitment.. 106
Commitment and Recommitment 108
Changing Your Way of Thinking with an Expecting End 114
Holiness in Sitting, Walking, and Talking............................... 118
Prison Letters 121
My End Thoughts... 124
The End 126
Prayers 127
A Prayer for you 129
Prayer for Addicted Children 130
Prayer When Our Children Disappoint Us 131
Prayer of Confession and Repentance 132
"Friends That Pray Together, Stay Together" 133

APPENDIX

List of Scriptural Sins To Be Read Before
    Confessing Your Sins In Prayer 137
What Do The Beatitudes Mean? 139
A Prayer For You And Your Family... 141
Order Form 144

Acknowledgment of Gratitude

I must start out with thanking my Lord for his continued support and love, for he was there for me when friends did not like me anymore. He was there for me when I did not know how I was going to make it the next minute, hour, day, week, month, and year. Thank you, Lord. I made it all because of you. In fact, being thankful for everything about my life has been one of my cornerstones of strength and resilience and has kept me going. I have many ways of showing gratitude especially in times of hopelessness or when a state of despondency threatens the core of my being and its essence.

My favorite ones are my songs of praise. "I thank God for those before me who went through similar things or even worse and made it through."

I would like to use this medium section to thank those individuals, church families, my pastor (Willie Wilson), copastor (Mary Wilson), Apostle J. M. Johnson Sr., Elder Esidore Gray, Rev. Mary Smith, Chief-Apostle Ann Savanna, Rev. Diane Griggs, deaconesses (Lavern Hines, Bridgett Turner, Elise Brown, Nadine), my son (Clinton Adams Jr.), my daughter (Dominique Gomez), my sister-in-law (Delia Hodges), (Aretha Williams, Rev. Ronald Hawkins Sr., Rev. Alva Rowe, Evangelist Joyce Thomas).

To the inmates behind prison walls, and other institutions that I may not have included, you all made it possible by supporting me when I needed your help and partaking in helping others realize their dreams. I hope our relationship was fruitful to you as well. I have mentioned just a few names here in this list, by no means exhaustive, of all those that help me succeed and not listed in any particular order of importance.

Jesus Christ. There is none like you. I know that I would not be who I am today and achieve this far without you—you are the greatest!

All the inmates that voluntary step forward with their life testimonies and not afraid of being transparent. I honestly do not think that this book would have been easy without all the moral and the assistance that they gave daily.

The staff of FPC Alderson, I would like to thank you all because you were my angels (my case manager, counselor, and my team manager) that were assigned to me. A job well done! God bless you all for your good deed.

I would like to thank my four wonderful sisters in Christ (Leslie Matthews, Crystal James, Bridget Bond, and Mona Lisa Gaffney). The role you played in my life over the past year is definitely proof that everything God does is for a reason. Thanks for all your insight and for letting me know that everything is going to be all right in the end. Thank you for believing in me and loving God's way. I thank God for providing me the opportunities to be a wife, mother, and a leader for God's people. God bless each and every one of you.

Thanks for all your sincere help and your true life testimonies for making this book a less painful ordeal. To those who rejected me—thanks a lot! It's God's inspiration that assists me to write, not man's alone. So no weapon formed against me shall prosper because my Lord God and his Son is with me.

DEDICATION

To my family

You are the best! If I were to enumerate the trials you have gone through with me and the love you have shown me throughout, your confidence in me has been great for my self-esteem. The only way I can summarize it here is—a woman's beauty lies in her God.

Thank you for being there for me when others abandoned me, for being my strength during my struggles behind prison walls.

I wish and pray that every woman will be blessed enough to share their lives with a family like you. I consider myself to be very blessed. It never ceases to amaze me that we have made it, despite all the external problems we went through. With prayer and fasting, we were able to stay happy while others who had few struggles watched their family fail.

Thank you for allowing me to be myself and for bearing my burdens when you did not have to. You have shown the world and me what a true family based on friendship, love, and, most of all, God should be. You are my role model. I hope you take these statements to heart; you have touched my heart forever. I love you all.

Special Dedication to Women

I am making a special dedication of this book to women everywhere in the world, particularly those behind prison walls; thank you for the contributions you make through every aspect of your lives. To all you women out there, I want to say if there is anything you want to do, you must find a way to do it. Never make excuses, no matter how legitimate those excuses may seem. This advice assumes, of course, that gratitude, happiness, joy, thanksgiving, appreciation, self-empowerment, *and* no procrastination through God's grace *is there*. And to the men in our lives, read this book to better understand our needs and help build us up so that we can better fulfill each other's needs!

Ladies, just keep on going and doing the right thing by all around you. I can tell you that even if man does not know and appreciate you for what you are worth, see 1 Samuel 25:35/ 41 or do, believe me, God knows. In his own time, he will reward you immensely in ways you cannot even imagine—even in your wildest dreams! I know because I have been there done that, as well. Despite what man did to me, despite thinking it was over, I perished, believed, stayed faithful, persevered through it all; and in the end, God showed his might. When God intervenes, no one can stop you or hold your blessing back, even if they try. When you leave prison walls behind, you can achieve if you know how. If you know what you really want out of life, no matter what has happened to you in the past or others have expected from you, you can achieve! To conquer adversity, you must first conquer yourself. God bless you.

PREFACE TO THE FIRST EDITION

God inspired me to write the book *Touched by an Angel*. The Holy Spirit has been prompting me to tell of my testimony in a written format. It is my duty to obey the Spirit and my ministry to let others know how good God is. I'm delighted to be sharing my testimony with you and especially to the struggling drug addicts and alcoholics. I want others to know how it feels to be set free. I was once in the same predicament, but thanks to God's grace and mercy, I have been delivered from both addictions.

My book will testify to how one day an angel of God touched me and instantly changed my life. The angel of the Lord found me hopeless, in despair, and a vagabond in the land. He touched and transformed me into a new creature (just like Apostle Paul in the desert). My eyes were opened to the truth, and I begin to transform into a brand-new person. I began to conquer sin and my many demons. I didn't do this on my own; it was by the work of the Holy Spirit. I remember giving my life to Christ, and the Holy Spirit took control of me and began to deliver me from the power of sin. God showed me how precious his blood was and how the blood of Jesus Christ was shed for my sins. The blood of Jesus paid the price for me. Jesus was the lamb that was stained for my transgressions, and up on the rugged cross was Jesus's blood for my righteousness. Once, my soul hungered for drugs, alcohol, and fast money; but now my soul desires God's love. I thank God every day for intervening and canceling Satan's plans on my life.

PREFACE TO THE SECOND EDITION

Jehovah Sermonettes is not a fiction or mystery; it is the true story of my journey. It will exemplify my happiest and darkest times. I will take you through some of my journal entries that will reveal some of my life's experiences as a child and as an adult. You will travel with me down my Road to Damascus and then up to the mountain of Zion.

PREFACE TO THE THIRD EDITION

Rising above Your Struggles is a life-transforming truth. You will come to understand my struggles as well as my walk with Almighty God. As God is my witness, you will read of my true life story through the present.

It is my hope also that my testimony will transform a life; bring spiritual revival to a backslider; deliver possessed minds, bodies, and souls; unveil the wiles of the devil and set the captives free; give conquering power over their enemies; and, most of all, bring salvation to a dying soul. I encourage you to tell others of my testimony, especially if they are lost or desperate.

PREFACE TO THE FOURTH EDITION

Behind Prison Walls: Inmate Number 27773-016 is my expression and experience in prison. During my wilderness experience, I had to rely on God like never before. It was my breaking point; God was then able to speak to me where I wasn't able to run. I tried boxing with God, but I soon realized my arms were too short to box with God, so I begin to let go and let God.

I believe others will be able to benefit from hearing or reading about my personal trials. I encourage youth pastors to contact me through my publisher to obtain a free copy of my book for their church library. In addition, anyone can contact me for a speaking engagement.

Thank you for purchasing my book; I am truly grateful. Your purchase will not be in vain. For it is by a divine appointment orchestrated by God. I hope you enjoy the adventure, and may God continue to richly bless you.

What Others Are Saying

To "Walk Your Talk" as a successful businesswoman is a challenge very few meet. Corvalis Hodges, walks her talk, is a successful businesswoman, and brings her wisdom and experience to all of us in a very readable and understandable form which originated from her experience behind prison walls. I encourage you to not only read this book, but to practice its principles.

—Sister Rita Taylor

This is a significant book. It covers key issues women face exactly like it is. Behind Prison Walls is a Christian book of encouragement for all women and men who are incarcerated. As I read it, I found myself challenged, stimulated and from my own previous imprisonment conviction. This book will be around for decades.

—Sister Bridget Bond

Corvalis Hodges is one of my favorite people. A Godly woman of integrity and high principle. This book is an excellent presentation of lessons which she has learned at her hardest side and in the marketplace. I recommend this book to Christians who are tired of just "going through the motions" spiritually and are ready for a healthier and more balanced life. Experience the rich, meaningful and abundant life available to true and faithful followers of our Lord Jesus Christ.

—Rev. Alva Rowe

This book goes right to the root of many of today's problems concerning healing and priorities of our lives. Besides nailing the issues on the head, it provides clear, substantiated answers from a biblical point of view. I think it is a must-read.

—Areathia Williams

I have seen Corvalis Hodges live this book. Behind prison walls, is not simply an expression of a woman's thoughts or opinions. I watch her go through, and I watch God bring her out. It is truly an expression of Corvalis Hodges' life. It is a must-read for anyone who would be a spiritually mature person.

—Rev. Ronald Hawkins Sr.

Dear Reader,

The book you are now holding has helped thousands of women find a deeper significance to lead more balanced lives.

This special edition copy of *Behind Prison Walls* is part of a unique effort to distribute a million copies to women throughout America.

A number of women made sacrifices for you to receive this book. Why would they do that? They sacrificed because the book changed their lives.

We live a busy life in stressful times. Many women have found an oasis of sanity in these pages. My dream is that, by reading them, you will find contentment in God, which really matters.

I would love to hear from you if this book has changed your life.

Please write to

> Corvalis Hodges
> 6207 Dimrill Ct.
> Fort Washington, MD 20744
> 301-536-7165
> corvalishodg@yahoo.com

Trust in the Lord with all thine heart and lean not unto thine own understanding. In all thy ways acknowledge Him, and He shall direct your paths.
—Proverbs 3:5-6

INTRODUCTION

All the women in this book are nonviolent drug offenders or white-collar criminals. Most are first-time offenders. The lengthy sentences they have received are real. They will spend their time incarcerated known by a number; in the federal prison system, they will no longer exist as people. Some of the women have twenty-year sentences, which for some means they will spend the rest of their lives in prison.

Today, many people complain about the double standard applied to traditional drugs, like alcohol and tobacco and illegal drugs, like marijuana, cocaine (crack), opium, etc. The *war on drugs* has created a counterrevolution in personal freedom. The martial law aspect of the war on drugs has done great harm to what were constitutionally protected liberties. Police in search of drugs come as invading armies in predominantly poor African American, Hispanic, and White communities. No longer does an individual feel secure in his/ her own home, or person. Mere suspicion is ground for an invasion of privacy. Once, our top priority was to be a free country, not a drug-free country. No reasonable free society has ever incarcerated more of its citizens than has the present United States. The war on drugs has turned a significant number of our citizens into criminals, with tens of millions of arrests for nonviolent offenses on the books.

Harsh sentences imposed on nonviolent drug offenders would be more suited to violent, antisocial criminals. Yet the federal government is exceedingly nonchalant toward violent offenders. In a federal court, a child molestation case carries a mandatory sentence of twenty-four months. Voluntary manslaughter carries a maximum of ten years incarceration, which is the lowest conceivable sentence the average first-time offender can hope for.

A major factor in determining who the government will pursue for drugs is money. While there are no funds to be harvested from prosecuting violent crimes, forfeiture law authorizes the government to seize money, vehicles, homes, and other assets from anyone remotely connected with a drug case.

UNICOR is the brains of the Bureau of Prisons, the agency that runs the federal prison system. UNICOR factories throughout the federal system generate over $400 million per year in revenue. Salaries and working conditions in

UNICOR factories are comparable with those in third world country sweatshops. One produces furniture, the other logs.

Most Bureau of Prisons staff at Alderson, West Virginia, are former army officers. The staff is trained not to see us as persons. We are not human beings in their eyes, but inmate objects. They despise us and make no bones about it. Prison officials tyrannize us and degrade us when they can. Strip searches do not function as security measures but as a form of humiliation.

Women who were shipped to a detention center to await transfer to prisons across the country were chained and shackled. Some of the women you are about to meet are now dispersed in prisons in all parts of the United States. The women you will encounter in the pages of this book come from different social, cultural, and economic backgrounds. For us, compiling the FPC Alderson Project has been an unprecedented act of public disclosure in the face of extreme injustice. Fear of retaliation by the bureau has been the greatest obstacle to overcome. Nevertheless, here we are, ready to let you in on America's dirty little secret. The statements presented here are unchanged from the day they were recorded. Reader, we ask that you read these pages with respect. Think of us as human beings, like you, not just names and prison numbers.

PART ONE

**The FPC Alderson Project:
Prisoners of the War on Drugs and
Breaking Generation Curses**

Inmate 27773-016

I lived in Oxon Hill, Maryland, where I conducted my business for five years. I am founder and CEO of my nursing agency. The company was formed as a sole proprietorship, which means, in essence, that the sole proprietor is the company.

I started my business with only one employee. Because my company grew so rapidly, I should have incorporated. Though my CPA had repeatedly insisted that I do so, I was too busy with my daily operations and, hence, paid little attention to what was really happening. As I later learned, this was a grave mistake.

Naively, I thought that every person that came seeking employment was honest. Soon, my staff expanded and consisted of slightly more than one hundred persons. Of the one hundred or so persons on my staff, ten gave false information on their employment applications and submitted fraudulent nursing licenses. Accordingly then, because I failed to incorporate my business, I was the responsible person, the sole proprietor. Because of my failure to incorporate, I was facing a sentence of up to fifteen years—fifteen years behind prison walls!

When this reality began to sink in, I pondered many questions. I felt like my life was over. As the days, weeks, months, and years passed, I began to inflict self-punishment upon myself and seriously considered suicide as an option, a way out. I felt that all was lost and deemed myself worthless and felt that I was worth more dead than alive.

At this same time, I was dealing with the shock that my daughter might be gay. That in and of itself was enough to warrant taking my life, or so I thought. Just as I was at my lowest ebb, the voice of the Lord spoke to me saying that you have another younger child that needs you; he has not acted out. He did not ask for this. Then, to make bad matters worse, I was trying to heal from a traumatic romantic breakup. So from January 2001 through March 3, 2005, I was in a dying state. I could barely function.

Out of the depths of despair, I began to fall on my knees and to ask for his almighty help. I know now that if he did not help me, I just didn't know what else to do. So I poured out my heart to God. I found some consolation in Psalm 142:107, which states

> I cried unto the LORD with my voice; with my voice unto the LORD did I make my supplication.

> I poured out my complaint before him; I shewed before him my trouble.

> When my spirit was overwhelmed within me, then thou knewest my path. In the way wherein I walked have they privily laid a snare for me.

> I looked on my right hand, and beheld, but there was no man that would know me: refuge failed me; no man cared for my soul.

> I cried unto thee, O LORD: I said, Thou art my refuge and my portion in the land of the living.

> Attend unto my cry; for I am brought very low: deliver me from my persecutors; for they are stronger than I.

> Bring my soul out of prison, that I may praise thy name: the righteous shall compass me about; for thou shalt deal bountifully with me.

You see, I was free, but my soul was imprisoned already. I was free to come and go. I was free to live. I was free to make sober decisions, but I had put myself into imprisonment. God stepped in and hid me. I did not know how I made it from one minute to the next, but I knew that God was carrying me because I was not able to carry myself.

I was led by God to fast for my first time for forty days, and after I came off the fast, the Lord led me back on one after being off for five days.

At that time, I returned to a thirty-day journey for the Lord, and after that, he led me back on another term. Soon, I realized that the year 2004 was over, and I was praising God like never before. Like never before, I was chasing after God's righteousness. It was not long before I realized that I felt relieved only during the months of fasting.

The year 2005 was now here, and I had to make 2004 a cornerstone. I appreciated the sentiment, but I knew that was all it amounted to.

Finally, I was sentenced to fifteen months. I wasn't happy or sad about the sentence, just relieved that it was behind me and that the pressure was off. I didn't have to make any more decision about anything else connected with business or my personal affairs. I didn't realize how I made it through when I was going through, but for the grace of God. I was stressed out and on the verge of a nervous breakdown. I fought for my life by fasting and praying. I pushed my way through by praying. I prayed until something happened.

When everything was happening, I promised that I'd get this straightened out, but God was letting me know that I was not in control of anything. Instead, he wanted me to call on his name. So I did just that! Jesus! Jesus! Jesus!

After being sentenced, I was able to self-surrender. I waited at home for the letter telling me where to report and when. This gave me a five-month period to get my affairs in order; this was a privilege granted to me because my spiritual father, my pastor, intervened and contacted the court personnel and negotiated this time frame so I could prepare myself for imprisonment. It pays to live right because God granted the request of my pastor. Five is the number of grace, so grace was just extended and unto me.

November 6 will always be a special time. For on that date, my family, friends, and church family came together and celebrated my early Thanksgiving; for on the eighth of November 2005, I had to surrender to the camp at Alderson, West Virginia.

During that celebration, we praised God as if it was the last day of our existence. You see, I had learned to praise God during my trials and my circumstances. I thanked God for going before, to pave the path before me, but most of all, I praised him for preparing me for my journey. When I told him yes, I then realized that journey was not about me; it was for God to get the glory through me.

God has prepared me for the worst; I had anticipated the worst type of prison. I had no idea whatsoever that I would be arriving at a prison camp that looks like a college campus or an all-girls school.

Upon my arrival at Alderson on November 8, 2005, my journey began. At times, I felt as though I was trapped into a time zone trying to find my way back. As I began this journey behind prison walls, invisible walls, I was no more my own person, my own boss; I, then, became another federal inmate with a number I had to remember. I had to remember that number wherever I went, i.e., to use the be bit tek machine, to use the computer, to send an e-mail, or to mail out articles; that number had to be used at all times.

The stripping process began immediately. My clothes, shoes, bra, panties, and identification were taken at the prison camp intake office, known as R&D. I was assigned khaki pants, shirts, old shoes, and a coat. When I arrived in my housing unit, an inmate gave me a pair of flip-flop shower shoes, toothpaste, and soap.

"They don't provide you with personal items," she explained. "You'll have to get those when your family sends in money to you." I then knew it was going to be a long night!

Little bits of decency were stripped away daily. "Bend over, squat, and cough. Stick out your tongue." I was told if I wanted to be seen by a doctor I had to pay a copayment of $2 per visit. That was a depressing moment!

At last, I mustered up the courage to ask someone where the church house was, and another inmate took me to the chapel the very first night I arrived at Alderson. I was amazed to see that chapel actually was a real churchlike edifice.

With all my attention focused on the pulpit, the visiting minister began to tell the story of Elijah's heroic confrontation with the priest of Baal on Mount Carmel. It may be difficult to believe, but as soon as the minister began to discuss Queen Jezebel and her threats, it brought this brave woman to her heels like a little scared cat! I broke loose and began to praise God like I was out of my mind; the separation from my family, kids, best friend was a rip into my very soul. I cried so hard that night after the service that three inmates came up to me and asked my name. It is awesome to see someone praise God the way you do. We have never seen anyone bring God in with them. Most of the ladies find God while they are here, but the difference is that you brought your God with you. I wished I'd never been born before I found God! Does any of that sound familiar? God asked me.

"But do you know what the angel said to Elijah?" the minister asked. "He asked him a simple question, and it is a question I am going to ask you tonight."

The people leaned forward to hear because the minister whispered the question in an eloquent soft voice, "What are you doing here?" Slowly, he looked over the congregation until he stopped where I sat on the second row. His eyes locked on mine. "What are you doing here?" he demanded. I couldn't look him in the eye. *You wouldn't believe why I'm here*, I thought bitterly. The minister's voice slashed through my thoughts. "I didn't ask, 'why are you here?' I asked, 'what are you doing here?'"

I glanced up. He was still looking directly at me. "Don't confuse the question with an accusation from God. It's not an accusation. God wants you to know that no matter where you are, no matter what your circumstances are, you still can make something meaningful out of your life. Hear the question! It's the most important question you will ever answer. And believe me, God expects an answer."

I heard the minister's words, but the reassuring content of his message got lost in the rubble of my own internal conflicts and bitter feelings. I understood Elijah's feeling a lot better, but I also began to understand God's question too.

I have always wondered about prison ministry, and I always wanted to be a part of the group. Then a still soft voice spoke to me and said, "Many are called but very few are chosen."

But the fact remains: people are suffering from lack of spiritual healing—not a mental one—not drug and alcohol addictions, and people will continue to suffer from this deficiency until they realize that there are divine laws of God and that God is the author of these laws.

We forget, don't we? that it is never God who fails; it is we who forget the divine purpose for our lives. God works through me, women, and prisoners to gain his objectives. True, God has often performed miracles.

Recently, I sat down with two inmates who have chosen to remain in relationships that pummel away at their spirits. Both women say that there is a reason why they are suffering and that their troubles are a test of their faith. After each conversation, I've taken to my bed for prayer because each one left me more devastated than before, by just watching women come to prison and look for other spirits just like them. Though they differ in age, race, background, and experience, both are smart, attractive, talented, ambitious, and otherwise no-nonsense women. And some profess to be churchgoing, and some maybe Holy Ghost-filled. There are lesbians speaking about improved family life. Some spoke on the lack of enough love from home, but the truth of the matter is the Word of God is . . .

We love Him, because He first loved us (1 Jn 4:19). When we as people fall in love with Jesus, Jesus teaches us to love ourselves. God doesn't require you to stay in this mess of life's frustrations. We all have a cross to carry. No cross, no crown.

I have heard virtually all the excuses women have given for remaining in abusive relationships, lesbian relationships, and for staying quiet and invisible for far too long; they rationalize staying in relationships far too long, for sacrificing big chunks of themselves to people and institutions and causes that devalue them as human beings. Daily, I talk to women who view their suffering and self-sacrifice as justified, just to have love and a relationship with men. There must be something God is trying to teach us, or God must really have something great in store for us to put us through all this.

No cross, no crown; the cross, the central emblem of our faith, is a symbol of suffering, pain, loss and imprisonment, and death. It is impossible to welcome this reality, but we must accept the reality, for we know that as painful as it is and will always be, prison is never the end but a new beginning. Through Jesus Christ, and thanks to his death and resurrection, we know that each and every day we suffer will result in a new beginning. The vision of new life, eternal life, the resurrected life is very compelling.

Romans 6:12 states, "Let not sin therefore reign in your mortal body, that ye should obey in the lusts thereof."

God has allowed the devil to test his people but has never left our side, not once. We have to get to a point in life that we are truly sorry for our sins; then, and only then, will God step in and mend our wounds. These are difficult times for the faithful. Upon coming behind prison walls, many feel battered by the inconsistencies of human interpretation of scripture. Repeatedly, I asked myself how ready we are, when we are in trouble, to beg God to help and save us, when there is nowhere else to turn, no other earthly avenue we can see that will lead us to safety, when we have exhausted all of our own skills and, perhaps, the skills of others to get us out of our predicament, we are very likely to call out to God. God alone.

This is OK because now he has our attention. We are after all only human. There is so much self-reliance can do for us when we are faced with terrible options or tragic consequences of the kind that may lead to prison/death.

I am tired of diagnosing people's problems, and now looking back over my life, I know people were equally tired of mine because, in the end, there is no cure but God because most of them do not accept the reality of a divine friendship or moral law.

When I am tempted with self-doubt and questions, my experience reminds me that God of all that I know and of those things that I don't know that I know. I am wondrously in tune with God's grace that lets me know who I am and who's I am. So many women in prison hide behind self-pity, drugs, alcohol, gay relationships, and low self-esteem to avoid doing what must be done and use you or anyone or anything as the rationale for their indecision or lack of action.

We do not honor God by inventing ways to stay in negative situations that cause us suffering and pain because our pain and suffering are nothing compared to Jesus Christ. Our pain is not about ourselves; it is all about God getting the glory.

We have to evaluate ourselves, how bad our situations are, and must consider how long it took us to get into them. Sure, everything has its ups and downs; but if your relationship, job, business, friends are weighing you down and if you are generally more sad than happy, it is time to do a balancing test and make some changes.

Stop waiting for a sign because signs may never come. Too many of us are looking for that sign. Release yourself! It's amazing how God can and will turn that thing around and open up the door to give you just what you need. You don't know what is in store for you until you get into a trial. Problems come to make you strong and to build your character. Your reaction to the problem will determine the length of time you dwell with the problem.

And it shall be, when the Lord, Thy God, shall have brought thee
into the land which he swore unto they fathers to Abraham, to Isaac,
and to Jacob, to give thee great and godly cities, which thou buildest
not and houses full of good things. (Dt 6:10)

Be pleased, O God, to deliver me: O Lord, make haste to help me.
(Ps 70)

There are many women that find themselves behind the tight jaws of the
prison system for various reasons; what they need is rehabilitation, but instead,
they are perfunctorily sent to see two types of medical practitioners: first for
trauma or stress. They are routinely offered sleeping pills or tranquilizers; then,
they are sent to the medical doctor or physician's assistant to give you a mock
physical, and again, pills like placebos are offered as the panacea for whatever
your aliment may or may not be. Many accept these freely given pills either to
get high or just because they are offered—not because they are needed.

I have had the privilege of seeing everyone that comes in because I am in a
bus-stop section, which where all new arrivals are housed before being assigned
to another housing arrangement. I have had to listen to the filth that comes
out these women's mouths, which has prompted me to share with them a book
that I read before coming to prison by Joyce Meyers entitled *Me and My Big
Mouth*.

My heart weeps for many women here at Alderson because they don't
know Jesus Christ, and they simply aren't trying to find him either. These are
holy grounds.

There are many that are nothing but made-up trash cans because the filth that
comes out their mouths does not make them acceptable to a decent group.

God has to bring people inside the prisons to commune with us because if
we were still on our jobs or on the street, he knows that we wouldn't give him
the time or day, so he knows how to slow us down. A dressed-up trash can is
a person that is physically well arrayed and looks lovely on the outside, but a
wholly messed-up concoction on the inside. Nice on the outside, but on the
inside you are all messed up. I know I've been there also, but today God has me
behind prison walls for many reasons so that I can share with the world that
it's not a nice place to be, but we are covered by his blood.

I will never ever grasp the concept of prison life because it is designed to
make you or break you. I had to humble myself when I came to prison so that
God could use me his way and for his glory to shine. How can one minister to
an addict and never been an addict? How can one minister to an ex-prisoner
and never been to prison? Although prison isn't for nobody, and I don't wish

prison on my (Maltese) dog, I mean nobody. There are some people who will leave the very same way they came in; they talk a good game for themselves to hear, but there's no footwork or change in their life. I don't mean that we will change overnight because I didn't. It was a process for me. I saw the change in me way before I came to prison, but it didn't change that; there was change before though, and when my season is up, the change would have been manifested, and many seeds would have been planted in other lives about the wonderful Jesus that we serve. Our God is the God that gives us chances after chances.

There are prison cliques. There are prison officers sleeping with inmates. There are women inmates sleeping with other women inmates. There are officers that look and act like men. There are inmates dressed and looked like men and have no respect for themselves or their cellmates. This is real stuff. The medical (HSU) facility is a mess.

HSU Alderson WV

Upon paying a $2 fee to HSU at sick call in the early morning, you would think that one of the nurses would see you for your problem. Think again, they will call your name, triage you sometimes, and tell you that you will be put on the call out in about two weeks to be seen for whatever problem that you have. No matter what problem may be, no matter if you have broken bones, no matter if you're blue in the face, their response is always the same: you will be put on the "call out" and we'll see you then. Imagine you having a broken arm or leg, you will have to sit around and wait two weeks just to see if you have either or. On many occasions, there have been times when staff members of HSU have given inmates the wrong medications to the extreme of having major seizures or blackouts. Some inmates on psych meds have been given the wrong medications, and the place wherever the person may be have to be shut down because the inmate had gone off on someone or went into hiding and refused to come out. There are inmates that HSU would up their dose of medications from, let's say, 150 ml-300 ml without allowing the inmates to gracefully go from 1 ml to the next, causing the inmates to have seizures that they never had before in their entire life. The inmates would drop right where they are; no one knows what to do because no one knows what's going on with this individual, not even HSU where she received her meds in the first place. How strange is that? Very strange, but here on this compound, it is something that happens on a regular basis, and no one wants to help or correct what's going on. To them we are just inmates doing time, not individuals who are in need of medical attention. Is there anyone that will help us, no? As much as we try to figure out who we can talk to, the more problems occur for all of us. It seems as though we will always be apart of this no-win situation here at Alderson, West Virginia. Will it ever change? We may never know unless someone steps in for all of us and helps.

On August 10, 2006, I received some bad news that my friend was dead. I just couldn't grasp the concept of that one because I just saw her two days ago. I knew that she had been complaining about her stomach for about two weeks, and every time that she would go over to HSU, the hospital would send her back and tell her like they tell everyone that they would put her on the "call out" and let her know when to come back. My friend Bell lost her life because of the negligence of BOP. She was forty-five years old, full of life; they told her the week before her death that she had gall stones but did not give her anything to remove them, but instead, they gave her pain pills. Well, the pain got worse and worse; she began to lose it to where another inmate was going to put a cop-out in saying that she thought that she was in limbo, not eating. And when she did eat, she could not keep it down, so at night the inmate would hear her throwing up. The truth of the matter is that she knew that Bureau of Prisons is letting HSU, the hospital, kill off people, and they aren't doing anything about it. On Tuesday morning, God touched an officer to make sure that she got seen and taken off the compound to a real hospital, and they kept her on Wednesday. She had surgery and passed away with a blood clot. This is not the first death that took place here at Alderson prison camp. She came in here one way, but they are taking her out in a body bag with handcuffs. She had three kids; one of her daughters is serving time at Danberry FCI. She was to join her mother in the month of September 2006. I don't see that happening today because her daughter is not going to come to a place where her mother died wrongfully. She had until 2012 to be released.

This death shook this place; everybody, all the inmates and officers, was affected by the death. I was messed up, and the voice that I was listening to was the Lord's. I stayed in prayer all day.

Today is August 11, 2006, and they are having a wait service for her. All I can say is that God is shaking this place. This has brought people to the Lord, but it should not take a crisis to come to the Lord. Thank God for your health, life, and your strength every day.

"You've been through some rough spots during the past few months, but you can't let it get to you. Things are gonna get better if you don't give up hope."

"This thing with your appeal may take a long time to clear up, but I believe you'll win in the end if you don't give up hope or lose your faith in God."

Everything had seemed so simple just six years earlier. During a relatively minor personal crisis at age thirty-eight after nearly a decade of struggles in my life. But I didn't have a clue.

Given the wreckage of my life at the time, admittedly hidden well beneath a veneer of personal and professional success, I should have seen disaster coming in some form. But personal tragedy is like the proverbial tornado that strikes in the dead of night: nobody expects it. We get up each day and go through the ordinary motions and routines of daily life, operating a business under the illusion that we're independent, self-sufficient captains of our lives. We assume that everything will go on as it always has—no matter how dysfunctional or bizarre—without interruption. For the most part, we're quite unaware of just how little real control we have or of how suddenly, drastically the trajectory of our lives can be altered forever either by external forces beyond our control or in combination with our own poor choices. I had a lot to learn about choices!

Behind prison walls, I've learned that

- no matter what happens, or how bad it seems today, life does go on, and it will be better tomorrow;
- regardless of your relationship with your family, parents, you'll miss them when they are gone from your life;
- life sometimes gives you a second chance;
- you shouldn't go through life with a mitt on both hands; you need one to be able to throw some things in life back;
- whenever I decide something with an open heart, I usually make the right decision;
- every day, you should reach out and touch someone. People love a warm hug, kiss, or just a friendly, encouraging word to brighten their day;
- people will forget what you've said, people will forget what you've done, but people will never forget how you made them feel; and
- I still have a lot to learn.

Satan came to kill me, and he was not playing around with the blows, or whenever he would strike, he would strike to kill. His résumé is to steal, kill, and destroy.

First strike was when I began to have the company issues with my employee's wrongful doings. Satan saw that I was OK with what was going on because I was not speaking about it, but I did say that I wished I was dead, so be very careful about what comes from your mouth because you can't take it back once it's gone forth. You see, I'd been poor before; and now that God had elevated me, Satan thought he could steal my joy by what I've worked hard for, and he was hoping that I couldn't live with myself because I was being broken down. I fell on my knees and cried out to God saying "Lord, if you don't help, I don't know what else to do."

Second strike was with my daughter coming out of the closet letting Momma know that she liked girls instead of boys! I didn't know what I felt at first, but I knew that I loved my daughter, and that was my seed that the enemy had his hands on. So I began to fast and pray because that was a blow below the belt, and Satan knew that if the first strike did not take me out, then the second one will. I felt like dying, but the more I prayed and fasted, I got strength. I battled with my sixteen-year-old daughter over boys, schoolwork, and her spending quality time with the Lord. I did my best to express my concerns regarding her well-being and spiritual walk, but it developed into an argument, and my emotions burst. Sometimes I feel hopeless as a mother and question my abilities as a parent.

Most parents of teens feel the same, so you aren't alone. And you aren't a terrible mother. Your daughter's simply becoming her own person. That's a good thing, but sometimes the process can be rough and sometimes painful.

Today my daughter is twenty years old, and may I suggest you adjust your focus from teaching your daughter to nurturing the relationship you have with her.

Trust God to continue speaking to her (them). As the mom of two, my favorite scripture these days is Isaiah 54:13, "All thy children shall be taught of the Lord, and great shall be the peace of thy children's peace."

When your emotions start bubbling over, remove yourself from the argument and calm down. Instead of fighting, pour your heart out to Jesus on a daughter's or son's behalf. Beg God to reach him or her, teach her, and correct her, if necessary. Then return to the room, listen to them with an open heart, and speak your mind with love and self-control. Then let go and let God.

Third strike was with a friend of mine because Satan knew that I desired to have a man in my life that would love me. Here's the truth, painful as it is to admit: Before I met the Lord, I spent a decade looking for love in all the wrong places. Convincing myself that if a man took me to dinner and spent money and time with me and don't let himself spend the night with me, he must (1) care for me and (2) think I'm pretty. Oh, the foolishness of youth! And the heartache after that of feeling unloved and unattractive. So I had to wear tight clothes to attract men "in the eyes of the beholder," when the Lord saw that you and me were not loved." Imagine it! Almighty God, the Creator of the Universe, looked inside a woman's broken heart.

The hardest thing to believe when you are suffering rejection is that anyone is noticing you at all and that you are being loved.

He cared for you and me. And God took away my pain as only he could. My last decade of looking for love ended when I found a heavenly bridegroom named Jesus. I soon discovered I had a world full of sisters, all of them beautiful. That includes you, sis! On those days when your mirror disappoints you, the "me" in your life don't affirm you, the children you have or don't have leave you feeling less than adequate as a woman, know that the Lord sees your brokenness, hears your cry for help, and can fill all the empty places with a boundless love that never ends. God and the Holy Ghost will keep you from falling.

Fourth strike was with my rodeo truck: all five lugs were about to come off, and the Lord told my friend to pull over and check all four tires, and on the driver's side, the front tire lugs were all loose and ready to come off. I would have lost my life if I had been driving that truck that day because I was in no shape or mind frame to check a tire. God's grace would not let me take the truck. That did not stop Satan's traps.

Fifth strike on my life was when I was to be in Baltimore, Maryland, for a book signing; and I drove my classic 1989 Jaguar, and as I traveled down the highway, I felt the steering wheel was very loose, so I prayed and I made it there. And when I arrived to my destination, the steering wheel was locked, so I was not able to move it. I had the Jaguar dealership pick it up, and they told me that I should have lost my life because they don't understand how I was still alive, and I got very quiet on the phone. Nothing but his grace.

I want you to understand something: The devil is real, and Satan does not play around with you when there is an attack or a death warrant for you. He will use whatever it takes for him to destroy you with God's plans for your life. Yes, I felt like killing myself; and yes, I felt like my world was over, but I also knew that God had a purpose for my life, and at times I did not know how I was making it because God was caring me when I didn't or couldn't care for myself.

Satan is cunning: he did not wait until one turmoil was finished before he would strike again; he kept on striking. So I had to gird myself up with the word of truth. Philippians 4:6, 7 says, "Be careful for nothing; but in everything by prayer and supplication with thanksgiving let your requests be made known unto God. And the peace of God, which passeth all understanding, shall keep your hearts and minds through Christ Jesus."

Took Place behind Prison Walls

Six strike was when I was tested again. I was sent a godly man that was living the Word and helped push me into my destiny. God had already delivered me from a married-man situation, but I lay awake at night asking myself how and why I didn't see through the lies and deception that was presented to me. Why? Because I could not see the trees for the clouds, and it was thick. My plate had been so full. I wanted to believe my friend because he was a godly man but in a fleshly body. I had to forgive him because forgiveness is for you; I can truly say that he did more good than harm to me because I can truly see because my eyes are open. And I am well resting in the Lord that he was not to be my husband; he was to just to help get me to the Son of God. When people come into your life, seek God's face for an answer why they are there, and he will show you.

After being on my journey for nine months, the truth started to reveal itself.

I had to give up my home, and because I was going to be gone for one year, I gave this man power. He stuck by me the whole while I was doing this journey for the Lord to let me make myself clean; the truth surfaced when he told me (1) that he was getting a P.O. box for the mail to come to and that didn't happen and (2) that he was staying with a friend of his and that didn't happen. The truth was that he had moved back home at the wife's house, and he had come forth with the truth because I could not understand why he didn't have a number for me to call him and an address for me to write him to. Codependence, I would say.

God had shown me the truth before the truth came out, so in a letter that I received and the wife's number was in it for me to call, I recognized the number right off, but I still put the number on my phone list anyway because I wanted to hear his voice. I called the number, and his wife answered, and I immediately had a flashback, and I asked for him, and she said that he wasn't home. That was the first attempt that I had tried reaching him. And on the second attempt, I reached his younger son; and after that second attempt, I wrote him a sweet, godly letter. Two weeks later, I received a surprise visit, and it was him. I loved this man and thought that he was my soul mate because we talked about marriage and began to do things, like spending a lot of time praising God together and knowing that he still had shackles on his feet and was taking me with him. I began to seek God's face on this situation and help him to tell me the truth, and the truth was that she was going to file for the divorce. Two years have passed by now, so God had to separate me to work on me. I began to reflect on life before I came to prison that, everything that I thought money could buy, God put up a stumbling block in my way because I was beginning to put this man's name on everything; but God said, "not yet." And I did not understand at that time, but today I do because I made a covenant with the Lord that nothing and nobody would hinder my walk with the Lord. I'm sold out for the Lord. I am being still, and standing on God is best for my life.

I am sharing this with you because God will allow the devil to test you in the area where God has delivered you from. I didn't bring myself out before, but for God, I would not allow myself to get caught up again. And this is how I know that God brought me out: I had a dream one night, and in my dream, I was a bride, and the groomsmen were waiting down the altar, but I could not ever see the groom's face. I thank God for molding me to be the bride that he has called me to be, submitting to (1) God and then to (2) authority and (3) then your helpmate.

After pondering my mind and speaking with the Lord about what should I do, God told me, "Be still and know that I am God. I will be exalted among the heathen, I will be exalted in the earth" (Ps 46:10). Today I'm standing on God, and he said, "Order my steps in the Word: and let not any iniquity have dominion over me" (Ps. 119:133). When you have done all that you can do, just stand and know that he is God all by himself.

I have made so many bad choices in the past, so I don't know what I want for me. I want what God has for me because I know that I cannot go wrong with his choices for my life. God will never take another woman's husband and give you to them if he is the one for you. The path will be clear before you, and nothing will hinder when it's time for God to bring two wonderful saints of God together his way. Psalm 119:11 states, "Thy word have I hid in mine heart, that I might not sin against thee."

Let me give you some of his attributes:

1. He is a Godly man.
2. He loves his mother.
3. He is a man that provides.
4. He is a man that doesn't give up during hard times.
5. He is a man that will pray with you and for you.
6. He is a man that pay his tithes.
7. He is a man with compassion.

He is my friend. God had released me from any pain, so I know that I am delivered by God; all things work together for the good.

Honestly, I was disturbed because just as I have made him my friend, I thought that I was his friend as well. Now, don't get me wrong. I know how hard forgiving people is. Man, when you have been hurt by people whom you love or whom you believed to love you and not to mention if they've hurt you more than once! Yes, it's a hard task to find forgiveness in a bleeding, broken heart. To move past the hurt and disappointment, when at times all you honestly want to do is hurt them, is a feat that seems insurmountable. But my sister, my brother, rest assured, it can be done. As a matter of fact, it must be done! God has called us to forgive our enemies, our friends, our family, and our loved ones no matter what they have done to us. Why, it just doesn't seem fair, does it? These people have pulled tears out of our faces, caused our hearts to be heavy with despair, and have even caused us to do harm to them and even sometimes to ourselves because of the unbearable pain that was inflicted upon us; and usually, we didn't do anything to them but love them! Ain't that something? Here we are all broken down, heart busted, can't see straight because our vision is clouded by our pain and God says "forgive them!" What! Isn't God omnipresent (all knowing)? Doesn't he know how these people have hurt me? That's all the more reason he commands us to forgive.

The scripture says that we have a high priest (Jesus) who can be touched with the feeling of our infirmities (pains/sicknesses)! And why is it that Jesus can be touched or moved by our hurts and pains? Because the scripture says that he was tempted in every point as we, but without sin.

You may say what relevance does this have to my situation? Well, God came to this earth in the form of Jesus Christ to reconcile man back to himself. Remember when Adam ate the fruit? Well, it was his disobedience that separated man from God and caused us all to be born into sin. That is why Jesus is referred to as the "second Adam" because, when he came through, the shedding of his blood fixed his and man's relationship that Adam allowed Satan to cause him to break.

Now, when God was on this earth in the body of Jesus Christ, he experienced each and every temptation that we humans have faced, but he did not fall into sin. He was treated very badly, he was betrayed by his friends, he knows what it feels like to have a broken heart, he has cried—did the scripture not say "Jesus wept"? He knows what it feels like to be dogged out, talked about, lied on, mocked, scorned, beaten bruised, used, and ultimately killed; you get my point? But as he was dying on that cross, he looked up to heaven and prayed for those who were hurting him and took from him, and he asked that they be forgiven because he acknowledged that they really didn't know who he was or what they were doing. They were shrouded in a cloud of ignorance; they were blinded by the devil, for if their eyes had been opened, they would have been celebrating him.

He was the Messiah, the true and living God! They would have been worshipping him and asking him to forgive them, but instead, they were killing him and laughing about it. What do you think happened to those people if they didn't one day repent for their actions? Yes, Ma'am, Sir, they will bust hell wide open. See, the scripture say (and I'm paraphrasing) that, in forgiving our offenders, we heap coals of fire on their heads!

Psalm 105:15 states, "Touch not mine anointed, and do my prophets no harm." Why do you think God would say that? He loves us; we are his anointed ones. Well, that's is why he also says that if you touch one of his little ones that you might as well tie a large stone around your neck and jump into the sea! Basically, God is like—I got this! That's why he says that vengeance is his! He doesn't want us hating and seeking vengeance on our offenders because it will only hurt us more in the long run. See, unforgiveness is a poison, and it can be mentally prison for some because it will only hurt and cause illness if left inside of us and eventually turn into a cancer—spiritually and sometimes even naturally—and that cancer will eat us alive until we are consumed by it, and it brings stagnation and then death into our lives! God wants us to forgive because forgiveness sets us free!

As long as we hold on to the unforgiveness, we bind ourselves to that person, making them God over our emotions. Jesus Christ wants to be God over our heart, mind, and soul. He doesn't want us in bondage to our hurt, disappointment, and pain. He came to set the captives free, not for us to stay in an emotional prison because we just can't let it go! Well, God wants us to let go and let God handle it. Yea, they hurt us, but God loves us and died for us and wants to give us life and life more abundantly!

My sister, my brother, God commands us to forgive these people mainly because he forgave us! We were low-down dirty sinners, and we hurt God on many occasions even in our saved lives, and he keeps on forgiving us! Who are we that we should actually hold a grudge and not forgive? Are we better than God? I think not! If we don't forgive, he said that he would not forgive us!

Sometimes we don't know how to forgive. We know we should, but we can't get it out of our hearts. This is what we need to do: first of all, repent to God for not forgiving and ask him to soften our hardened hearts that we should be able to forgive these people and move on with our lives. Now, we don't have amnesia, so we will not forget the things that they did to us, but we will not hold it against them either.

Ask God for his peace in your heart concerning these people and pray for their salvation if they are not saved. Ask God to loose you so that you may let it go. You have things to do for God, and you can't have anything holding you back from your destiny. Understand that, just as the people were persecuting Jesus, they didn't know who he was, neither did these people know the anointed man or woman that God has created you to be. Forgive them, Father, because they know not who they are messing with! If they don't change and repent, they will reap coals of fire on their own heads. I had to ask God to set me *free*. Ask God to break those chains over your life that you might be set free. Who the son sets free is free indeed! If you have to scream, cry, run, jump, dance, roll on the floor, or silently hold yourself and rock back and forth, just allow the Holy Spirit to have his way. Call on his power, his anointing, his strength, his peace that you might forget those things that are behind you and press toward the mark of the high calling, which is in Christ Jesus! Old things are passed away, and behold, all things have become new! This is a new day in Christ Jesus. I'm no longer bound by the pain of the past but free to pursue my destiny in the future.

Now that you are moving toward the future, do not go backwards. Forgiving someone who has continually hurt you does not mean getting back involved with them to be set up to be hurt again. God calls us to use wisdom. If someone means you no good, then they are to be dealt with a long-handled spoon. You've forgiven them, you pray for them, and you deal with them minimally, if you even have to deal with them at all. If you know they haven't changed and are not willing to change, then the best thing to do is to leave them in God's care. He knows how to handle them best. But you don't want to be hindered in any way of reaching your full potential in God.

I am praying that this testimony has helped you tremendously to let the hurt go because God doesn't want anything or anyone to come between you and him. The rapture could take place at any time, and we don't want be left down here, but we want to be caught up to meet him in the air. This has been a test for me also. I love you and really care about you, so be encouraged and keep holding on to God's unchanging hands because he will bring you through.

I'm forty-four years old, and I'm starting over. Although I've been working since the age of fourteen, I have no real savings, except the saving that I started in prison because I was used to saving. I still have my retirement funds. I've entered a debt management program to pay off my credit cards and to raise my credit score.

Working through the poor choices I've made in the past, it feels as if starting over at forty-four is late, but having two of the most important possessions—your health and the courage to want to change—will ensure that things will turn out favorable on your/our behalf.

Getting your balances paid off earlier will help you in your stride to have a peaceful life. As you pay off your debts, your credit score will increase, and your debt falls, and a higher score means you'll be able to qualify for whatever your heart desires.

Although a high net worth can make life less stressful, it won't help with your self-worth. I want you to forgive yourself; we all make mistakes. What you do to change your old habit is a sign that you have the strength to build a better life, and we know that "all things work together for the good of them that love God, to them who are called according to his purpose" (Rom 8:28).

Everything that has happened to us is an opportunity to learn. You're clearly on a path to mastering that lesson and finding the greatest treasure of all: a person you're proud of. I shared this with you to let you know that God is still in the business of blessing, as you go through any wilderness experience that will rise up against you.

During my dying state of my life, wondering why I was not drawn to seek to drown the pain through misuse of drugs or alcohol, I remember thinking back then that I could better understand why people seek escape in so many ways other than reaching for God; and somehow deep down inside, I must have known that the point of the desert was not to escape it but to press my way through it, leaning heavily on God's presence and almighty power.

When the trials and wars of life hit, I remember whose care and guidance got me through—no, better than getting me through, he tempered me, tested me, totally provided for me—and I now can rest in that strength and am full of faith through the angry storm raging. Why me was the question so many ask themselves, but my answer was why not me. Though the desert sand and wind was blowing in my face, I remember the tender, compassionate God that I met in the wilderness; this is where it all began for me. God birthed me spiritually in the wilderness; I gave birth nine months, and nine months is the number when women give birth to a baby, and somehow, I am better prepared, by his loving hand, for war because war cries, not in my own strength, but merely by leaning on him and asking "Which direction do we head, God? What shall I think, feel, say, do?"

The wilderness—definitely worth the trip. I have seen all kinds of things happen in the wilderness and all kinds of oppression happening here. Satan is not happy with me.

God took the children of Israel, and myself personally, through a wilderness experience, a place where sufficiency was not found in the surroundings of the day. Jeremiah 2:6 describes it in the dakes as "the land where no one travels and no one lives." It felt just like that, the land of death and despair, realizing that I cannot do it myself, the land of-out-reach self-sufficiency. The mantra that sang its way through my head so often (I can't do this) ended up being true only if I tried to do it on my own strength and resources. But being there in the wilderness, I learned that, when leaning on God's breast and communing, the wilderness takes on a new meaning: it no longer matters if I can't do it. It only matters that I am there with God and that he is fully capable of walking me through it, somehow delighting in the fellowship as we walk, crawl, cry, or laugh. Exodus 13:17 states that God did not lead the children of Israel through the most direct route of the place he promised but took them through the desert (the despair-ridden, hard, seemingly pointless, excruciating long, winding, sand-filled path) because he had a greater purpose than just getting them to the promised land.

He was preparing them for war. So I often said and thought, *This is so very hard, beyond my human strength, being away from loved ones, children, and church family, but, most of all, being isolated, set off.* I cannot cope at times, and then reading these words in scripture, I can begin to appreciate and rejoice over God's ways that are placed over our life, clearly not my own. He chose a difficult, seemingly impossible long path.

I do not seek to be melodramatic but to look back and say, I get it a bit more fully today and want to learn more of God's purpose . . . and I would say now that God has chosen my path and your path through a hard place in order to prepare us for what is/was ahead.

He lovingly had to put to death my people-pleasing because, left to my own devices, I'd have continued to seek to please people rather than God for the rest of my time on earth; and he knew that would set me up for failure, so he began to toughen me up and teach me to lean on him for counsel and not be swayed so much by what another thinks, bringing me lesson after lesson after continued lesson of nudging me to speak up and tell the truth and let the friend fall or rise, depending on who could walk and stand on God's word, a walking vessel for the Lord. My life has been transformed and I will never be the same. The wilderness was definitely worth the trip.

I remember saying years ago that I wanted to get into prison ministry and a little old mother of the church said to me "Honey, you did not tell God how you wanted to." I must say that you must be careful about what you speak. Proverbs 18:21 says, "Death and life are on the power of the tongue: and they that love it shall eat the fruit there of." It can produce death or life. Proverbs 15:4-5,7 says, "A wholesome tongue is a tree of life: but perverseness therein is a breach in the spirit. A fool despiseth his father's instruction: but he that regardeth reproof is prudent. The lips of the wise disperse knowledge: but the heart of the foolish doeth not so."

The God that we serve looks on the inside, and man looks on the outside.

We got to admit that we haven't been all that we should have been, but thank God that you are not where you used to be. God looked beyond our faults and saw our needs.

"Delight thy self also in the Lord: and he shall give thee the desires of thine heart, commit they way unto the Lord; trust also in him and he shall bring it to pass." (Ps 37:4-5)

I found joy in the midst of my failure; when we are able to do that, then we are well on our way. When we go through a period of intense disappointment, remember this moment of Christ. Turn from the failure and then thank God for that which he has made possible for us to do. Not only will the one failure be left behind, but we will be able to recognize and appreciate those areas, which God has intended to bless and which he has already prepared for us.

Perhaps we are working among people who, because of pride and spiritual arrogance, cannot accept Christ's precepts. Don't fret; there are others who are searching and who will welcome your words. I have come to appreciate what it means to be grateful when people do things for you even if you paid them to do it for you; showing genuine appreciation can and will bring out the best in people and has a way of harmonizing a situation that could have been chaotic.

Showing genuine appreciation to people can really make the world a better place, in prison or out of prison. I thank God each day for a new day and ask him to "order my steps in thy word: and let not any iniquity have dominion over me." (Ps 119:133)

Having a second chance at life is an honor. I appreciate this journey from the Lord behind prison walls. I could not have made it in the wilderness if it was not for God; God hid me in his secret place. "He that dwelleth, in the shadow of the almighty" (Ps 91:1), God will protect you if you trust him to guide you. My advice for you is to let God use you and don't be afraid. He is the only way. Be a vessel everywhere you go; I wish you all Godspeed.

PART TWO

CHAPTER 1

Inmate Number 18530-018
Lois Dell Fait (white women)

I lived in Florida nearly all my life and have always been a law-abiding citizen. When I found out that my mother was dying of cancer, I moved to Roanoke, Virginia, to help care for her; there in Virginia, my whole life took another course.

I met a younger man who led a different lifestyle than I. He introduced me to a woman that had a past history of drug involvement. Together, the two of them introduced me to a totally different way of living. I still don't quite know how it happened, but one thing just seemed to lead to another. The woman got busted for selling drugs and after that needed a place to store her drugs. This younger man I was dating talked me into letting the woman keep the drug at my house. Whenever the woman needed some of the drugs to sell, she would come by, pick up what she needed, and my boyfriend would get some drugs for his own personal use for storing the drugs at our house. Looking back, I realized meeting this younger man was the turning point in my life. My mother had just died; this younger man was paying me lots of attention. I was very vulnerable at this point in my life and looking for love in all the wrong places. It seemed I couldn't help myself when it came to him; I would do anything he wanted.

Well, one thing led to another, and I started selling a little drugs here and there. One night in February of 1995, I got stopped in my car by the police. They found drugs and proceeded to tell me that they know I was working for this woman, and if I would tell them everything. I knew they'd let me walk out scot-free. So I did; I told them what they wanted to know. I went back to my house with the police following me, and they recovered the drugs out of an old car that was in my backyard. I fully cooperated as they had asked.

I continued living at the house for a little while but finally came to my senses and decided to get out of this life. I packed everything up and moved back to Florida in June. Four months after the incident with police in Virginia, I received a phone call in Florida from the police. They wanted me to come back to Virginia and help bust the case against the women and others involved. They promised

I would only receive a couple of years in prison. At this point, I was scared; I knew I had already gotten out of everything, so I told them I didn't know what they were talking about. I guess I shouldn't have done this, but I was scared and didn't know what to do. Then in October of 1995, the police came and arrested me, and I went to jail and was charged with *conspiracy* to *distribute cocaine*. When I went to court, my lawyer said if I didn't take a plea bargain to ten years, then I would probably receive a life sentence. So I agreed to a plea agreement of ten years, but ultimately received eleven years and three months.

I've been in prison for approximately ten years now. I am seventy-four years old. Since I've been here, I went to work in UNICOR, the prison industry inmates, where I made approximately ¢46 an hour. I worked there for about five years of operating a drill press that makes holes for furniture, and many more. There were no guardrails that accompanied this machine. One day, my hand got caught in the drill press and smashed my left hand. I received $55 a month for a year under workman's compensation and still only have partial use of that hand. I had never been in any kind of trouble, but for the first introduction around drugs, I will pay for that mistake for eleven years of my life (well, more than that, considering I still have to complete five more years on paper for supervised release). I believe this punishment is harsh, but that is the law. I will be seventy-five years old when released from prison, and this is what they call justice.

Chapter 2

A Testimony for the Lost and Found

My name is Lisa, Lisa. I can see now that all my life I've been running from Jesus. Jesus kept up with me and saved my physical life many times than I know of; I'm sure there are many I don't know of. I use the name Lisa, Lisa for a reason, and that reason is for my safety and my family's safety.

Everything caught up with me one evening. I came to the end of the line. See, several years before, I was baptized as a satanic priest, and part of the ritual is to blaspheme against the Holy Spirit. So when I finally hit rock bottom, I prayed to God.

I said, "Lord, I'm tired of being in prison. If this is all I have to look forward to because of what Mark 3:29 (NLT) says, 'But anyone who blasphemes against the Holy Spirit will never be forgiven. It is an eternal sin,' then let me die. If there is anyway you can forgive me and have a plan for me then please let me know."

Then I made a rope from my security mattress and knotted a noose. I wrote a message to my mother, "I'm sorry. I love you," on the wall; then I climbed on top of the sink, put my head through the noose, and stepped off into space. Satan had me, and he wanted to make sure he kept me.

Even though it is written, "Do not test the Lord your God" (Lk 4:12), I almost died, but God showed me mercy. I had lost my bodily function, and death was near when God broke my rope. The material the rope was made of was very strong and thick, and there was no way it could have been broken except by the hand of God. When the rope broke, I fell nine feet headfirst onto the concrete floor. I didn't break my neck or fracture my skull but did have a deep cut that lost a lot of blood and needed stitches. I was taken to the hospital emergency room, and while there, a correctional officer said, "Maybe God is trying to tell you something." A miracle, yes, it was. It was an act of God.

It was last June that I accepted Jesus as my Lord and Savior and was baptized.

I'm a totally new person. I no longer take medication for depression and anger control. I no longer look at or read immoral books; I no longer harbor hate in my heart. The Lord is making many changes in me, and it shows by my actions. The biggest thing Jesus has done for me is giving me eternal life.

Thank you Lord for your mercy and grace, for without you, I would be lost. Praise God!

* * *

Hi, my name is Michell, and I am from Detroit. I came into prison with a heart as hard as stone; my life and all I cherished seemed to be gone. I didn't care about time or the light of day; I was a drug dealer from Detroit all the way. I didn't want to smile and didn't want to talk; there was nowhere to run and a small area to walk. I was around hillbilly boys and Mexicans too, but when it came to Detroiters, there were very few. There were Muslims, Christians, and devil worshipers about; there were muscle women, skinny women, and some women that were stout.

Each day I awakened to look at prison walls; everybody that was around had tattoos and scars. I've always been a loner and a self-absorbed person; I try to avoid trouble just as much as I can.

It's been said that the Lord works in mysterious ways; he has been right in here with me through these terrible days. He guided me past stabbings and walked me around fights. He's carried me through hard days and slept with me in lonely nights. He's helped me detain my anger and kept me out of trouble. He's returned my husband into my life, so our love can unfold.

He's opened up my eyes so that I can finally see, and even though I'm still in prison, my spirit is finally free.

(I've been locked up for forty months with eight more to go) Praise the Lord, I praise him high, I praise him low; and I shall praise our gracious Lord everywhere I shall go. May God bless all these who read and decide to give God a chance to change their life and situation around.

CHAPTER 3

No-name Testimony

I'm just an ordinary woman who had extraordinary problems. My life has been plagued with every kind of sin imagined. There was drug addiction, many types of crime sprees, sexual immorality, and total disregard for all types of authority; and the list goes on. I lost my husband, two beautiful and loving children over drugs. I lost good jobs and even good businesses. Went from profession to profession, relationship to relationship, always looking for that happiness inside, but never found it. Then I lost a real good job in 1996 and turned back to drugs and went back into crime again.

Then one early afternoon in December 1997, I found myself surrounded by a group of FBI agents and sheriffs with guns to my head. I was being arrested for a federal crime. So many things went through my head. I knew that there was a possibility I would never get out. My whole life just fell around me. Now handcuffed and strip-searched and feeling very lost, I saw no light at the end of the tunnel. As I stared out the window of that cold one-woman cell in a jail awaiting extradition, I felt hopeless. I knew of this Jesus Christ but really did not see what he could do for me, such a wretched person as me. Thought I was too bad for God. Little did I know what a plan he had for me.

There was an inmate who invited me to a Bible study that next evening. I went and listened to the word of God still tossing this born again thing through my mind.

Let me tell you, I surely was a broken woman. As the Lord says in Psalm 147:3 (NIV), "He heals the broken hearted and binds up their wounds," I was soon to learn this. As the time passed shortly by, I did confess as in Romans 10:9 (NIV) "that if you confess with your mouth, Jesus is Lord, and believe in your heart that God raised him from the dead, you will be saved" and Romans 10:10 (NIV), "For it is with your heart that you believe and are justified and it is with your mouth that you confess and are saved."

Now that the Lord Jesus Christ is my Savior, there is a tremendous load lifted off of me. As God promises comfort, so now I have that wonderful feeling

I have with God, and surely I've found that inward peacefulness, that inward feeling of freedom.

I was sentenced to a term of twelve years, but that doesn't matter because of knowing that I have a God that is loving, merciful, kind, and always there. God is doing time with me. If God sent his only begotten son to die for all our sins, he surely loved the world. You can find the same freedom from bondage of sins like me. Make the most important step of your life and accept Jesus Christ. Accept him as your Lord and confess your sins before it's too late. Live your life for Jesus Christ and be set free. If God can give me inward freedom in a federal prison, just imagine what he can do for you.

Since I wrote my testimony, the Lord Jesus Christ has been moving in me. As the Bible says in 1 Corinthians 6:19-20 (NIV), "Do you not know that your body is the temple of the Holy Spirit, who is in you, whom you have received from God? You are not your own: you were bought with a price. Therefore honor God with your body."

Now I daily carry my cross because I love Jesus Christ for myself so much that I owe my life to him. James 4:7 (NIV) says, "Submit yourselves, then, to God. Resist the devil and he will flee from you." The blood of Christ has cleansed me, and indeed, I'm free.

My charges were reduced, and I was released August 2006. I'm free, indeed. Thank God Almighty, I'm free.

Chapter 4

My name is Tanecia Carter. I was born to Rosa Carter and Victor Ray. I was born in Richmond, Virginia, on September 12, 1978. I'm twenty-seven years old, and I have one sister named Tanecia Carter and no brothers. My mother and father got married when I was eight years old. When I was growing up, all my cousins either lived with me or were around me all the time.

I was a problem child growing up. My first time ever getting into trouble was when I was in the Head Start program. A little boy tried to take my milk from me, and I hit him in the head with my chair. My fighting with boys was on a regular basis and did not stop until I got to middle school; because I got too old to fight them, I started to like them instead.

When I was in the sixth grade, my mother and father separated, and we moved from the house that we lived in since I was in the first grade. Not long after we moved, my mother got a new man into her life. One day, when I was cooking, he was picking with me; I put the fork in the hot grease and took it out and burned him with it. He didn't mess with me anymore after that.

By the time I was in the eighth grade, we moved again to an apartment near the projects. This is when I first saw somebody get beat down to the point of seeing blood coming out of his head. I saw a boy got knocked out with one punch. It was the projects where I learned about sex and a lot of fights. I really thought I was bad until I moved by the projects. My best friend could not come and visit me there, so we began to separate. At one point in time, we stop talking over a boy, but I told her we were better than that to fight over any boys.

In high school, I started to have boyfriends. My first real love was in high school, and he died in 1996. I went to visit him, and by the time I got there, he had been shot only thirty minutes before I arrived. He got shot four times for a coat he had on. By the time I made it to the hospital, he was dead. I blamed myself a long time for his death. If only I had gone to his house, maybe he would not have been in the wrong place at the wrong time.

One year later, I got raped. This young man bit me so badly on both sides of my face and arms that the scars still show today. I had to go to the hospital because my face was swollen. The next day, my mother made me go to school; however, that day I had to do a presentation in front of my class. That was the most embarrassing moment for me in my life. The whole ordeal was traumatic enough, but to have to stand in front of the class with a swollen face was more than I could take. The coldheartedness of the teacher angered me, to think that they wanted to videotape me.

The next year, I was skipped from eleventh grade to the twelfth grade, but I was required to take two English classes. To add to my anger, I had the same teacher that videotaped me and embarrassed me badly. I tried to get into another English class with a different teacher. I tried to get help by explaining to the principal why I was so traumatized by the English teacher, but he has his own issues going on where he could not hear a word that I was saying, so I dropped out of school. That's when my dreams of being a lawyer were crushed.

I bought my first car at the age of nineteen, it was a '98 Oldsmobile. I loved that car, but it was a lemon; it worked for four months and then broke down on me.

I had another death. My cousin was getting high, and a dude came in and shot him in his head. My memory of this incident was awful. I went to visit him in the hospital to see him, and his head was very swollen. I couldn't even tolerate looking at him. The next day, they pulled the plug on him, and he died. The same year, I lost another close cousin. He was killed by one of his friends who shot and killed him in his car as he robbed him for drugs.

I was still nineteen years old, and in the same year also, I was raped by an old friend that I knew most of my life. He wanted me, but I didn't want him, so one day he came into my sister's house while she was on the porch. I thought he was cool, so no one thought anything about it, and he came into the house and took my sexual rights from me.

At the age of twenty, that's when my marijuana addiction was very bad. I smoked every day and night, when we went out to party or just hang out. The point is, I really smoked a lot.

When I turned twenty-one years old, I was seven months pregnant. I had a son, and his father and I were not together. They say, "What's been done in the dark will come out." I began to sleep around with other guys or cheating. My friend forgave me, but I couldn't forgive myself for sleeping around, so I stopped going out with him. I was eight months pregnant when my mother and I moved to Maryland. I was on my own, and I got my own place. I had a new boyfriend until "baby momma drama." Since we decided to stay together, the drama began one day when his baby mama needed some things. She did not respect herself enough, so she could not respect me in my house and would do anything to get him, but I begin to see myself in the mirror. Later on, she came back while we were sleeping and broke in; I dragged her out and called the police.

My drug addiction was beginning to get real bad. After that, I was smoking 'cause it made me feel good; it made me feel better. I could chill and have fun.

I packed up and moved again, but lo and behold, this is where I caught my drug charge. I was always around where I was seeing people lose their life getting robbed and shot up at times; I have been close as five feet away. Friends would not visit me because of where I lived.

I would never, ever have thought that I'd be locked up. It took twenty-six years to get here, and here I am. April 2005 was the beginning of my nightmare that was to be known as my life. On that day, the police came into my home, searched, and found a shotgun, cocaine, and a firearm. I stayed at Richmond City Jail for two-and-a-half weeks before I got a bondsman. The bondsman was to take me back to the city jail because the marshals had a hold on my bond. When I went to court, the state dropped all my charges, and I had to wait forty-eight hours until the federal government sent the marshals to pick me up. I received four indictments. I received a bond that meant that I go into my aunt's house, and she tried to take over my life. She was very tight with me; she would not let me go out to wash clothes for my kids, so I went any way, and she called my probation officer. I went to court, and she told the judge that I could not stay with her anymore, and in November 2005, I got locked back up until my court date in December 2005. I pled guilty to a charge of maintaining a place for distribution and storage of a controlled substance, and the judge gave me twenty-four months (two years).

I began my twenty-four months at Northern Neck Regional Jail. While being there, my grandfather passed away in January 2006, six days before his birthday. My grandfather was like my father; I could talk to him about anything.

I'm in the R-Dap program and trying to get my life together, and I believe God has given me a second chance at life, and I am taking advantage of this opportunity. I just want to thank God and my role model and mentor, Ms. Hodges, for always giving me a word from God and a word that gives you hope if you just let God do it for you. Ms. Hodges, you were like a mother that I needed on the outside. I respect you and every word that came forth. I will get into church and let God use me.

I thank God for keeping me alive to tell my story. God bless you all.

CHAPTER 5

Inmate Number 56234-083
Pastor Shaunna Watson
From Stronghold to Strength

I write this to completely expose the unmitigated gall of Satan to try and destroy the work of the cross concerning my deliverance. It has certainly been given to the daughters of Abraham to possess the land; be strong and courageous, for the Lord our God will never leave us or forsake us. However, through the wiles of the enemy, I was lured into sin. Notice, I wrote *lured* not *lead*. But the faithfulness of God was with me. This spoke directly to the harassing spirit, which sought to take my family, ministry, and life. You see, the enemy questioned every area of my integrity and character. Now, during this inquisition, I was found guilty through the kingdom of darkness. The devil had sent out a search warrant with the highest level of risk attached to the warrant: armed and extremely dangerous and shoot to kill. You see, sisters and brothers, it is not that you can't get it together; you have been lured into a trap, so the enemy can get you to abort your baby, which is your testimony, deliverance, and miracle. Consequently, through my moment and my misery, God had placed a miracle in my life. So for at least two seasons in my life, I had my misery, my moment; and then God granted me my miracle! He allowed that devil to be delayed so I could escape! He began to speak to me concerning my stronghold through the scriptures. 1 Samuel 22:5 spoke very clearly to my spirit, saying, "Do not stay in the stronghold depart, and go to the land of Judah." I was so overwhelmed by this powerful revelation I began to speak to everyone who was in distress, disconnected, and distracted. Whatever the discouraging situation was, I spoke life over my situation, and God brought it to pass! The Holy Spirit began to deal with me to let his people know lust, greed, and pride comes from the adversary. I had been delivered because God saw the plans of the enemy, and he blocked it! God began to show me his anointing was the hedge around my life. Now after being delivered, I stand on the scripture, Daniel 11:32, "but the people who do know their God shall be strong and do great exploits." Now my confession has made my life an example of how God will never change his mind concerning the calling and gifts to the people of God, for he uses us to usher the rest into the land. Much like Paul, I didn't want to write to you with excellence of speech or in the wisdom of man but in demonstration of spirit and power through the testimony of Jesus Christ and him crucified. According to Romans 10:13, whoever calls on the name of the Lord shall be saved. This not only means salvation but it means you can begin to walk in your deliverance, healing, and miracle for you and the family. Stay encouraged!

In him,

Shaunna A. Watson
Pastor and Evangelist
56234-083

CHAPTER 6

Testimony

First and foremost, I want to take a moment to thank God for this opportunity to stand before you sharing my life. I should have been dead years ago, but for the Grace of God, I'm yet living to share my testimony with you. My name is Inez Lindsey.

I was born and raised in Detroit, Michigan, at Herman Kerfer Hospital to parents Isaiah Sims and Louella Mercer. At the time of my birth, I had one sister, Barbara Mercer, from my mother's first marriage to Lonnie Mercer whose last name we all carried until my mom and dad joined together in matrimony in 1964. I don't really remember much up until I was around seven years old—then it was seven more kids. My mom stayed pregnant; she had twenty-two children. We all were stairsteps, so at a young age, we were responsible for each other. I remember spending a lot of my time with my grandmother on my mom's side.

Other than that, I was my father's pride and joy. He was my heart; he was tall with pearly white teeth, black as the night, and very, very handsome. He was soft-spoken, never raised his voice, but had zero tolerance for nonsense or foolishness. He was a hardworking man for a construction company, also a chef prior to that for the U.S. army.

Mom was half-and-half; her hair was down to her buttocks, and she was built like Betty Boop. She never had time to work because the babies kept coming, but in between pregnancies, I remember her being a barmaid. My dad didn't want her working anyway, so he kept her pregnant.

My grandma on my mother's side was a God-fearing woman; she loved her some Jesus. There were twenty-eight of them. My great-granny, my grandma's mother, lived with her; she was old and set in her ways. I used to love to be over my grandma's house because whoever was first to go to Great-granny's room and help her was rewarded a dip of sweet Garrett's Snuff and a small glass of Black Label beer; so know that I was the first in her room whenever possible. She didn't drink water; she said that she was allergic to it, so all her life, she drank beer instead. She died at the age of 114. All except maybe five of her children were alcoholics: you just drink; it wasn't against the law.

At my granny's house, we went to church every time the church door opened. We learned how to cook, clean, iron, and wash. There at home is where we went to school from; education was first priority. After all chores and homework were done, we were allowed to go outside and play with other children.

My oldest sister was very sick because, at the age of eight, she caught a cold; and the live germ from the cold ate a hole in her heart. And they didn't have the medicines and knowledge back then as they have today. So it cost a lot of money for her medical care, but with much prayer, my sister lived twenty years over what the doctors had given her. She was so pretty to me, bowlegged, built like a brick house. I thought the world of her, and I wanted to be like her. Everyone loved her; she got a lot of attention. I guess looking aback, knowing what I know today, you can say I was jealous of her. I would do things like work extra hard to get attention or crazy stuff like steal change from my granny and plant it on my sister so she could get in trouble (she never did though). I would always get busted in some kind of way. Her friends were awesome; they dressed sharp, went places where I wasn't allowed to go. But I would sneak anyhow; I was curious and bad. Away from being around adults, I was like the bad seed. In front of them, I was so innocent.

I remember coming home from school one day, and our furniture was sitting outside; we had gotten put out. I saw my father coming home from work with his friends that he usually rode with. This time he didn't stop; he kept going. Our world would never be the same. My mother took me and my brother over to my father's parent's house, and the rest of them went to my mom's parent's house. The next time I saw my father was about two weeks later, picking us up to take us to our new home, which was a two-family house fully furnished upstairs and downstairs; you could smell the newness throughout the whole house. My father was now selling drugs; he vowed his family would never get put out again. Before long he was one of the biggest pimps and dope men in Detroit. He started an organization called the East Side Twelve, which was the largest pimp and drug men in the city of Detroit. He had boosters, prostitutes, B and E boys, and hit men on his payroll.

At nine years old, I was wearing five hundred outfits to school. At thirteen, I knew everything there was to know about making money. My father didn't live with us anymore; he had his own place for our protection. He was very protective of his family. He became the godfather of Detroit, and no one messed with Dank's kids or wife. Kids didn't want to play with us because, I'll just say, kids are cruel; they would say things like they think their family is better than us, which was far from the truth.

Yeah, we were not a bad-looking bunch of kids, and none of my brothers and sisters thought we were better than anyone else. All I wanted was to be a part of, so since they wanted to play rough, I started manipulating my way with money. I started giving away my diamonds, telling my dad I lost them. I began taking lots of money to school, buying my newfound or, should I say, newly bought friends whatever they wanted. I had my own crew now, so my big sister was not an issue to me anymore. I began sneaking and hanging out with gangs, drinking wine, and skipping school.

The teachers thought I was crazy because I would only come and stay in school on test days. I was a straight A student; I never studied. You could read one line to me out of a book or show me one math problem, and I went from there. I could just do it. On weekends I would stay over my granny's house, go to church, sing in church; we had a group called Frankie and Her Pride and Joys. I'll talk about Frankie later, who was my mom's sister; but after my granny died, my mom had to legally adapt Frankie, Lillie, and Netta, her three sisters who by nature are my aunts, but by law are my legal sisters now.

So I had two different lifestyles. My grandmother died at the age of forty-eight and as a result, church went out the window, but the seed was planted in my heart. I know today that there was a covenant over my life through the prayers of my granny. I remembered as I got older in my addiction that I would always sing a song that my granny taught us as kids; I'd be drunk walking the streets at three or four in the morning alone, trying to cop drugs, singing, "Walk with me lord, walk with me." I don't know why, but I did.

My mom would send me to my father's a lot because she saw straight through me. I was stealing, lying, skipping school; so my punishment was to go stay with my dad. And that's exactly where I wanted to be. I was the only one there getting spoiled rotten. All my father's friends became my uncles; the prostitutes became my aunts. I was raised by them; they taught me the things they felt were necessary to make it in this world as they saw it. The booster made sure my wardrobe was intact. The prostitutes and pimps made sure I had money, and the dope men made sure I knew what dope was. Their philosophy was dope was made to be sold and not used. If by chance you use, use it; don't allow it to use you.

I remember one day my father got a disturbing phone call from my mom. He left, and that was the last I saw of my father for seven-and-a-half years; he shot someone for disrespecting my mom and was charged with first degree murder, an imprisonment of seven-and-a-half to fifteen years.

After that I didn't see too much of my uncles and aunts; it seemed as though, since my father was gone, they forgot about me. I became angry, mad at the world, and I was going to show these people what I was made of and who I was. I went back to my mom's, taking my father's drugs and money with me also. Only giving my mom the money, I was keeping the drugs I needed to get and fit in the gang I'd soon be part of.

My oldest sister got a job stripping to help with bills; I started hanging with her. I was her responsibility. I would sit backstage, and it was beautiful watching the men throw her money. And in the lights, she was the center of attraction in my mind. The doctors had her on morphine and dahlias; I watched her skin-pop herself. She had not a care in the world. Now I started stealing her meds to get high on, sneaking out of the house, stripping while mom was at work. I'd end up giving her money.

Though I grew up real fast, I was still angry at the world because my father was gone and no one seemed to care. I remember the riot breaking out in Detroit around 1967; the army was posted in my school, which was across the street. One of their tanks was in our front yard. Then I was introduced to guns. Lots of fellows came over our house; my mom welcomed them. They showed us how to load and unload guns and rifles on their lunch break, and I was taking it all in. I remember telling the people I worked for I was twenty-one when I started stripping, but I was only fifteen. I knew how to make false IDs. One of my uncles did that, and he taught me.

At one of the strip clubs (burlesque), I ran into Texas Slim, one of my uncles. He took me out of that club and gave them the flucks, telling them my age at that time was eighteen. I felt like I was grown; Moms had no control over me, so he gave me a job waiting tables at his club. I found out that the reason they weren't in my life after my father got arrested was because some of them went down with my dad.

Now I began drinking heavy. Uncle Slim sent a guy to pick me up from work whom I fell in love with. I became pregnant by him, and that's when I got introduced to heroin, for he was a heroin addict whom they named Bugs Moran. He was so fine he reminded you of a young Bill Dee with an attitude, a killer mentality. He's the father of my daughter.

Let me go back; after my dad went to jail, I got pregnant with my son whose father was also a baller, I didn't tell anyone because my sister was in love with him. So I started dating his younger brother, who died in his sleep. He died thinking that he was the father of my son; the real father denied him until he was killed by his wife, who was my cousin. As for my daughter's father, Bugs, I caught him in bed with one of my sisters. I was devastated; heroin became my best friend.

My children stayed with family; I was just sleeping there. After I came in, I'd be so drunk or high I couldn't do nothing but nod or sleep. When I woke up, I'd be so sick, and all I could do was to tell my children I'm sorry I was a mess. I began staying away from home at long periods of time because I didn't want my family to see me that way and kept making promises I could not keep. I was staying from house to house with men that really cared about me. I couldn't receive love; I wanted them to hurt as I did. I would turn them out on drugs and go my merry way; I kept a job at a strip club or a-go-go bar. Tips were good and so was the pay. No one really messed with me when they found out who I was.

I met a guy name Alfredo Lewis; he was crazier than I. He was a stickup artist. We would go from town to town sticking up people, gas stations, stores, bars, dope men, after-hours joints; it didn't matter whatever we thought of. I was on a death mission. He accidentally shot me in my leg. I overdosed in the hospital while I was in traction. I was crazy after leaving the hospital; they put a fifty-pound cast on me from my breast to my ankles because my thigh was broken in six places. But that didn't stop this addict; I continued robbing and sticking up people, not caring that I couldn't run nor bend. Al was arrested for robbery; I wasn't with him that particular day.

I went back home; my mom put me in a methadone clinic. My father came home; finally, my life was going to change. We went from rags to riches again in a matter of weeks. A month later, I found my dad and brother dead, both shot to the head. I went on a mission to destroy and hurt everything that came in my path, including myself.

In 1977 I met my husband; I turn him out on heroin and coke. I put the man through pure hell; he held onto his job: he worked for the postal service. When he came home one day, I was laying on the bathroom floor with the needle still in my arm. He called 911; they pronounced me DOA. I woke up downstairs in the morgue, not caring I was in a strange place or what had happened. I wanted to know where the rest of my dope was; my husband sent me to my final rehab.

In there, this lady was telling her lead; she said she prayed to God until her knees was bleeding. Something in the way she said it, I knew it was hope for me. I went upstairs and began to talk to God. I said, "God, this third step tells me to turn my will and life over to the care of God as I understand you. Well, I don't know or understand you, but if you just help me, I'll serve you." I was tired to the point I couldn't do nothing for myself when I arrived at the rehab. I weighed 89 lbs, my eyes were set back in my head, my skin was gray, you could see the skeleton in my chest, I was dead. After I finished talking to God, I knew it was over; I was not the same person who got on my knees.

Upon leaving, my husband was still drinking and using coke. An old running buddy of mine who I used to stick up with, my sister in crime, came by my house; she heard I was out. She took me to church. I later found out she was now a missionary. God delivered my husband and began to bless us exceedingly and abundantly, more than I could imagine. I fell in love for the first time; he removed the stony heart and gave me a heart of flesh. I was able to cry and forgive; I was saved.

There are a lot of things that I don't remember because of blackouts; I can remember, though, my body waking me with the shakes, needing a drink, and racking with pain because I needed heroin. I can remember selling my soul to the devil for a puff out of that pipe, but in the midst of it all, he didn't let me die. I thank God he allowed my mother to live long enough to see me saved, ministering the word. I walked out of my season for the love of money and allowing the devil to use the love I had for my family. I'm not blaming no one for me doing what I've done, but I'm glad that he allowed me to come to this place where I can learn about me, myself, and I, a place where I didn't have to be ashamed of where I've been. I thank God for all of you, the drug treatment staff, for being understanding to my needs. The past I can't change, and I'm not proud of it, but thank God, he kept me in the midst of it all. Again I thank the drug treatment staff for looking beyond my faults and seeing my need.

CHAPTER 7

Inmate Number 12848-171
Dawn Vaughn White (Stepmother)

My charges were embezzlement, and I was facing thirty years, but God stepped in and gave me a favor in my life with four months [left behind a husband *that she* had been married *to* for one year and two months, *an* eight-year-old stepdaughter, *a* mother, *a* sister, and a fourteen-month-old niece. When I received the sentence to leave, I found out that my mother was dying of cancer of the lungs. The week before I left, they took my mother back into the hospital.

Question: How do you feel about not being by your mother's bedside?

Answer: I don't know how to answer that, but I pray every night before I go to bed, and I ask God for his loving protection and for God to send his angels to watch over my mother until I'm able to be there. This is the only thing that is taught on me. My prayers are that I will be home when God calls her home to glory.

My advice to anyone: if you are considering embezzlement, don't do it because it is very hard on you and your family. I am twenty-seven years old, and I am very grateful to life and my God. And most of all, I thank my family for their love and support because there are many girls, women, mothers here at Anderson, West Virginia, that don't have family. It makes you appreciate the little things that life has to offer. I will continue to seek God's face when I leave this place with God walking and talking with me. What Jesus did for me not only declares my present but it prepared a victory. Sometimes there are some disturbances in this present life; there are some things that all of us at some time are not so happy about.

I don't know anybody else who will stand by you like Jesus. I don't like to get hooked on things. I like to know that what I'm holding on to is able to suffice. In God there is no weakness; there is no failure in God. You don't have to worry about a letdown. The strength of our faith, the strength of those things that God has designated for us, continues to flow inside. We say, sometimes, nobody loves me like God; nobody cares for me like God. I thank him for the suffering that I had to endure. I cherish knowing that, everything God did, he did it for me. The Bible says David encouraged himself. You think about what you got, what God has declared, makes you feel good. I know he didn't bring me in behind prison walls to make me sad but to get the glory.

> He sent his word and healed them and delivered them from their destructions. (Ps 107:20)

CHAPTER 8

Inmate Number 18765-058
Lavanda Moffit

Quick decisions can cause disasters and the cost may be high. If we acknowledge God in all our ways [in the workplace, home, the community, wherever] he will direct our paths (Prv 3:6)

[Inmate number 18765-058's charges were embezzlement.] I was facing thirty years, but by the grace of God, I only received five months, with two months behind prison walls and three months home detention.

After waiting for the court to punish me, I had already punished myself with the long drawn-out agony; the "wait process" is very painful. I confessed on August 2004 with my charges. In December, two weeks before time, my biggest mistake was not sharing it with no one. I went to court back and forth by myself. Nobody in my family knew about the trouble that I had to deal with. I shared it with family on the day of my sentence. My husband knew about the trouble, but he was mad with me and the world. My husband hoped that the problem would go away, but up until the last month before I left, he changed his life, and our marriage started to heal. This was a new beginning for my marriage and my life with God. My purpose in life, I feel, is that I must turn everything over to God and let him take care of my worries; and everything else will come next. My embezzlement was addiction; I was addicted to gambling, and I couldn't find my way of stopping on my own.

Have mercy upon me, O God, according to thy loving kindness; according unto the multitude of thy tender mercies blot out my transgressions.

Wash me thoroughly from mine iniquity, and cleanse me from my sin. For I acknowledge my transgressions: and my sin is ever before me. (Ps 51:1,3)

God had to step in. I went to Harris Casino to gamble, and at times I went every other night in Turkey, North Carolina. I hit the jackpot for the amount of \$163,000 at the casino. I maxed out all my credit cards and took from our household account/bills. My husband knew about the problem because he was there every step of the way with me. I played poker/shamrock. I played four-dollar bit every night. I hit the jackpot in less than fifteen minutes. I love gambling, but it did not love me. This went on for nine months. I embezzled money from the bank in the amount of \$56,000. I told on myself I was the bank manager and they never knew about the money that had been missing over nine months. I had embezzled the money. I'm a shame.

Question: How do I think prison has changed my life?

Answer: I hope and pray when I leave behind prison walls that I can go back into society and hold my head up high, by God's grace and mercy!

I hope and pray that this testimony will help just one person because gambling is just as bad as crack cocaine. The fear that I had coming to prison was the unknown. I am rejoicing and glad; my heart will be encouraged to continue to fight the good fight of faith. God bless!

"For in time of trouble, he shall hide me in his pavilion." (Ps 27:5)

CHAPTER 9

Hi, my name is Andrea Patton. I was born on March 30, 1986, in Lexington, Kentucky. I was raised in a broken home by my single mother; she struggled hard to provide for her five children.

We lived in a small house in Lexington, Kentucky. By the time I was eight, we moved to Louisville, Kentucky. There my mother met the man who would be the father that I needed. Things started to get better for my family. My mother was happy; also, my siblings and I were happy. We stayed in Louisville a little over a year. Then we packed up and moved to Detroit, Michigan.

We had been there for about five months when my stepfather passed away one night. I was up watching the late-night Gary Coleman show. I went to try to wake my father up because that was our favorite show. I kept pulling, pushing, and calling his name. He didn't move; I got upset and awoke my mother. She then pursued trying to wake him and started to panic! I watched helplessly as she performed CPR. My oldest sister or somebody then called the paramedics. I sat there on the side of my father, watching helpless, as he began convulsing. My mother steadily performed CPR while he was vomiting. When the paramedics finally showed up, I figured he had passed away. As they left to take him to the hospital, I heard my mother say he was gone.

Over the short years that I had Steffan in my life, I grew to love him unconditionally. He was the father that I never had. His death really impacted me. It was even worse for me to lose him because I couldn't attend the funeral. My mom thought that I was too young!

We moved back home to Kentucky after his burial. I was never the same. I became depressed, rebellious, and out of control. My mother tried to help me with counseling, but I didn't think that I needed help!

By the time that I turned twelve, I was in trouble with the law. I was put out of public schools for my behavior and conduct. I was sent to the juvenile detention center on several occasions for shoplifting, assault, harassment, disorderly conduct, and a list of other crimes.

On February 14, 2002, I gave birth to my first son. His name is Lejuan Hutchinson. He was the light that I needed to see. He changed my life dramatically. I no longer went out shoplifting or getting into trouble. I dropped out of school in the ninth grade to be a full-time mother. I enjoyed being there to cater to my son.

By the time he turned one, I was a heavy marijuana user. I didn't realize it then, but the marijuana was changing me. I become a very moody, mean, and paranoid young lady.

My mother and grandmother used to tell me that I needed to stop. I ignored their warnings.

One morning, I woke up and decided to go shoplifting. I got caught, and I served twenty-eight days in juvenile lockup. The day that I was released, I gave God my word that I'd never smoke weed again. That night, upon my release, I was tempted. I was tempted to smoke weed and fell to it.

I got pregnant with my second son in September of 2004. During most of my pregnancy, I continued my drug use.

During my second pregnancy, my brother was tried and convicted of a firearm. He was sentenced to five years. After his sentencing, I tried to pass the bar to hug him. I knew that it was going to be a while before I could hug him again.

He had been in and out of jail for eight of his twenty-one years. During his lockup periods, I barely got to visit him. He is my best friend. I love my brother to death. I will do anything for him. Well now, I'm at the end of serving my five-month sentence for trying to hug him. I do not regret doing what I did in the courtroom that day. Although I do regret not listening to my mother and grandmother's advice, not only was I incarcerated, but I lost temporary custody of my children because of my drug abuse.

I believe that the Lord is putting me through these obstacles to better myself. He wants me to turn back to him. He wants me to leave the drugs alone and to depend on him.

Since the death of my stepfather, my life has spiraled downhill. I've made a promise to myself upon my release from Alderson Federal prison camp; I will leave the drugs alone and fight to get my babies back. I'm giving my life back to Christ, getting into school, and starting over. I've been reborn and want to make this life right. I want to walk, talk, and live righteously, with the Lord's help.

CHAPTER 10

Inmate Number 27260-016
Candace

[For possession of a firearm during a drug traffic and perjury, Inmate 27260-016 was facing thirty years, but God stepped in and gave her twelve years. I had to ask myself the question.]

Question: How did it make me feel not to know that my life could be over with thirty years facing me?

Answer: I really did not think about my time, but all I thought about was I wished and I could have and should have, but did not.

Question: Who did I leave behind?

Answer: My son who is seven years old. I was held in jail for two years before coming here at Anderson, West Virginia. Prison is not for me.

Question: What have I learned from this situation?

Answer: My family is the reason that I am here with twelve years. My boyfriend is my reason for me being here. I had his coat on, and I lived in his home, and the police came with a warrant for his arrest.

Question: What would I say to young women and young men at the age of twenty-three?

Answer: Their association could get you into a lot of trouble, so I would say just choose who you affiliate yourself with and around. I could not choose my friends because of poor choices, and today I choose to live and be around positive people. Today I have not heard from my boyfriend that put me in this situation. I had no choice but turn to God. I had no love from home, and I had no guidance that two people would give you, so I look to a man in the street. There is nothing that God has declared that he is not able to accomplish. I lied, I cheated, I sold; but God saved my life. I believed if I was still home, I would be dead.

The word of God does not just give you a beginning of a situation; it declares the end of it. Sometimes in the middle of the process, we don't see the end, and you got some situation that you just don't see the end visually. But you got to know that God has declared a beginning and an end of that situation. Inmate number 27260-016 believes the ultimate end has to do with God's accomplishments. God's got everything under control even when it doesn't look like it. When things are all haywire and moving in every direction, God is still monitoring the situation. When I was home and on the street, I did not go to church; but today I pray, and I am very remorseful. I was young and just out of high school; my life was ahead of me, but I thank God that my life is not over. Today is the beginning of my life. God's word has already spoken in my life. God's words have been spoken in your favor. Stay in school and listen to your parents. Don't act like you are the parent. I will be thirty-five years old when I come home. Kids pay for their parents' curse all the time if the curse is not broken, so I have asked God to break the curse off my kid before I have any in Jesus's name.

Know who you are connected too, and with 27260-016, making the right choices is very important. I am concerned about God's word today, and God is concerned about my situation. "When my father and my mother forsake me, then the Lord will take me up" (Ps 27:10).

CHAPTER 11

Inmate Number 36777-007-171
Vida McDowe (black)

I was quietly slipped into the Alderson, West Virginia, federal prison camp to serve out a twelve-month sentence for an escape charge after being watched.

I should have been dead after everything that I had to endure. I began my life at the age of fourteen, and today I am thirty-five years old, and I have really been through so much in my life. I got arrested at the age of thirty-one years old, and I weighed 130 pounds. I got locked up in Washington, DC, and was place in CTF. I have been on drugs all my life. My drug of choice was crack cocaine. I stayed in a house wherever I could get it. I got high at hotels. Every charge that I ever got locked up for was drug-related. The drugs had gotten me so bad that I thought I was a superwoman and that I was invisible to the world, and all I contemplated was on how and what I could get from them. I did not stop until I got locked up. I was faced with charges before me, eight warrants for my arrest. I had seven misdemeanors and one felony.

I left behind a praying mother and three children: one beautiful daughter and two sons. When I got arrested, I felt relief in my spirit because I was tired of running. As I was being arrested on Sixteenth Northwest, I began to look around because I knew in my heart that I was looking at some hard time. I feel this time that God has paved the way for me because the devil would have taken me out of this world, but today, I am blessed and I am grateful to God for a second chance at life. Now, I am at peace about what's gonna happen to me.

I know that everything the devil has taken from me has already been replaced by God through the abundant blessings he gave me. When I leave this journey, I will live a better life because I owe it to God first and myself, and I owe it to my kids and family. I am still alive today to live and to share this testimony with the world because of my mother's prayer.

I was sitting at McDonalds one day, and I saw this guy getting a house; my stomach began to flip inside out. I had a lot of money in the bank, and I had been clean for thirteen months, and I knew what I was doing was wrong.

I kept fooling myself, thinking that it was ok, and the money was gone; but I was never told that it gets worse each time.

I had my daughter in my mother's bathroom. I had just finished smoking a fifty, and I thought that I had to use the bathroom, but I was in labor. After giving birth to my daughter in the bathroom, I got the afterbirth and wrapped it up and put a maxi pad on. I then called 911 to inform them that I just had a baby, and so the ambulance arrived at my home in seven minutes. From that point on, I have never taken care of her to this day. I really don't know who she thinks I am to her. I don't know whether or not she thinks that I am her mother or sister, but she looks identical to me when I was at her age of five. My oldest son knows that I am all their mother, but my two youngest kids don't know who I am. I have some explaining to do when I return back home.

I graduated in 1988 from Oxon Hill. My aunt took me to Baltimore, Maryland, to a party; and that's where I met my son's father. After one year, I went to visit him and I bought a bus ticket at Greyhound bus. I was in love, and I lived with him for seven years. We went through our breakup, and I moved to Wheaton, Maryland. My son's father was self-employed, and he was five years old when his father died. My husband-to-be was taken away from me suddenly by lightning. He was self-employed; he was a roofer, and he got struck by lightning. He was twenty-eight years old when he passed away, and I was twenty-six. After my husband-to-be passed away, I lost it from that point on. I was well provided for, but the money went like water. This was the very beginning of my end when I first got high. I was alone and feeling alone, but deep down inside, I really was not alone (Psalm 23).

Chapter 12

Inmate Number 22599-057

I sit here with Inmate number 22599-057. Inmate 22599-057 came behind prison walls at the age of twenty-eight. Inmate 22599-057 came behind prison walls very upset because she just realized that she wasn't going anywhere for a while, that prison would be her new home for the next ten years until God says differently.

Inmate 22599-057 left behind her family: mother, father, husband, and three beautiful kids. I asked various questions to Inmate 22599-057:

Question: I asked Inmate 22599-057, what did you do for man to give you ten years?

Answer: Inmate 22599-057 was selling drugs; crack cocaine was her selling choice.

Question: When selling drugs to people, how did that make you feel?

Answer: I sold weight, and I really did not think about what it was doing to people.

Question: Did you think that you would ever get caught?

Answer: No, because I looked at it like it was a job, but I have done a lot more things than sell drugs and didn't get caught then. I am paying the price today for the old and new.

Inmate 22599-057 feels that her kids need her, but she's not able to be there physically. "I know that I done wrong but now I'm paying for it. Now I have so much time to think about life and my kids because we were very close. I sold drugs to take care of my kids and to live the good life. There wasn't a day that went by that I did not shop." Inmate 22599-057 said that her past is eating

72

away at her "because a sin is a sin any way that you look at it. I had to ask God to forgive me for my sins. I still ask God for his forgiveness; forgiveness is to deal with."

Inmate 22599-057 said that she loved her husband at times more than God when she was at home and living in the drug world. "But God stepped in and said to me, 'Let me test this love affair.'"

Inmate 22599-057 said that she is mentally tired. "Tired of all the hustle and bustle." God came into Inmate 22599-057 in a dream with handcuffs, and he told her that he was sending her a warning, "but I didn't listen, and he knew that I wouldn't listen. I felt that I had to go and make that last sale, because of my greed."

"My greed is what got me here behind prison walls." Inmate 22599-057 said that God stripped her of everything, "all the material things, except the most precious things that I did not think about: my husband, my kids, my mother, and father. Today I am spiritually free, and on the inside, I have peace that only God can bring." Inmate 22599-057's plans for the future is to feed her mind with positive things and to read his word and to get a closer relationship with God and let God use her for his glory. Inmate 22599-057 feels though that "God saved your life. God saved me from myself. I'm free now because I was headed for self-destruction. I got a mandatory sentence and that means you have to do that time no matter what. A long old friend was the one that turned me in, someone that I knew for eleven years; and my friend started to use drugs for her own personal use."

Inmate 22599-057 tried using various drugs such as weed and the ecstasy pills, but never crack cocaine. The ecstasy pills came in different colors, such as pink, blue, white, etc., and all shapes; but most of them are round.

Inmate 22599-057 is very remorseful about her past life. "The thought goes through my mind, *How can I help the next generation?* and that is by me telling my story to the world. If God changed me, I know that he will change other drug sellers. There are so many other thing to do in life, and money is not everything. I was told by the officer in Winston-Salem, North Carolina, that they were going to make me out an example. I had no bond. I'm dealing with a trust issue today: I don't trust people easy. All the greed and the money was not worth going to jail or prison for."

"Today my life has changed; I will never be the same again. Today I'm saved, and I'm trying to live holy for God. Today I just want to help people and tell my story. God sits high, and he looks low, and God sees all what you are doing at all times. Today I appreciate life and the simple things."

CHAPTER 13

Inmate Number 068
Carrie Williamson

My charges are conspiracy charges. I was in someone else at home, which they had been watching for years, and I did not know 'cause I was there at home doing hair when the police came with warrants. I was facing twenty years, but God stepped in right on time and touched man's heart, and I received one year, six months.

I thought my life was over because the thought of me leaving my husband, daughter, my three sons, and my mother behind was the devastation part that was most difficult for me.

I was very upset about it, and I am still a little upset. I cannot get comfortable, and the hospital care is very bad; they don't seem to care about the inmates here at Alderson, West Virginia, at all; but listening to other inmates, this is not all bad either.

God has placed Sister Corvalis in my life here at Alderson, West Virginia, and I thank him for that because I love what way she is—and that I mean. She's so peaceful and spirit-lead. She helped me to want to live a better life when I leave. Sister Corvalis's words are "God didn't put your future in the hands of somebody. He didn't make somebody in control of what's going on in your life. This is God's business." Whatever God has declared, the enemy can't do anything about it. I know he is kicking; he is trying everything. So it is a continuation of learning how to trust God that is important in our relationship with God—my past, my present, and my future. God has already declared it to be.

Being here behind prison walls is something that I will never ever forget. It is a place that I don't want to come to visit short or long term again in my life.

I know that I was Corvalis's assignment from the Lord because she said that I was torn up from the floor up. I thank God for her because, many days, I don't think that I could have made it without her guidance in the Word and her prayers that help me not run away. It bothered me at first when I used to hear her tell another church person that she was on vacation, but later I had to learn that God had her there for a reason, and he was still working on little old me. I did not have peace when I came to Alderson, although I was at self-surrender. I did trust people before I came. I'm learning that I was in control of nothing, and life is going on without me. Don't think you are by yourself, and don't get down on yourself. God does not remove us from the realities of life. And I think that one of the things that trouble us in our walk with God is that, when we are experiencing realities of life, it's only a test. I have learned in prison that there are two things that you don't mess with and that is another "woman's woman" and another woman's "food."

PART THREE

God Will Make a Loser Win

I'm tired of doing hard time,
With no reason.
So I'm happy that God found me,
Who's good in anytime or season!

I've squandered my whole life,
And thrown it all away,
But still the Lord Jesus
can mold me just like clay!

I've been in many jails and prisons,
Where most of my life's been spent,
As Satan has deceived me,
But by me, this, it was not meant.

I tried hard in my lifetime,
I've cried a million tears;
Oh my life it has been wasted
Down through all the years.

Sometimes I hide my face,
And in my cell I cry;
How could I not believe the truth,
And exchange it for a lie?

So now I pray to God for Jesus,
Thanking him both night and day;
Yes I thank God for Jesus,
And for showing me a better way.

I feel him in my heart and soul,
As he's always on my mind;
Remember Jesus is here to help us,
Whenever we get in a bind.

Following the Lord Jesus is simple,
But it is not easy you see.
Though for the cost of following Jesus,
Always you'll be free.

Free from the shackles and bonds,
That keep us chained to evil sin;
For if you stick with Jesus,
God will make a loser win.

Now if I go to heaven,
I'll be looking for you up there,
Because we have the perfect peace of Jesus,
When we're under his loving care.

TREATMENT

I'm writing this poem in hope to rhyme about the real reason people are doing time. It's not that easy to explain you see, I have this problem called dependency.

Over drinking and drugs that I can't touch, It's not that I don't like 'em, I like 'em too much. Even if I smash the bottle and flush the crack, there's still behavior problems that keep coming back.

I need to grow up over emotional lines, so I can be a strong woman and really change this time. I have two children who depend on me, another big reason to want treatment.

I can't do it alone, I need a lot of help; so I get on my knees and humble myself. "God help me please." God has entered my life and given me hope and power to live without the crack cocaine.

I'm learning to stand on my own two feet; so I can be a good daughter, wife, mother, and finally return to all that I had.

LETTING GO AND LETTING GOD

To let go doesn't mean to stop caring, it means I can't do it for someone else.
To let go is not to cut myself off, it's the realization that I don't control another.
To let go is not to enable, but to allow learning from natural consequences.
To let go is to admit that you are powerless, which means the outcome is not in my hands.
To let go is not to try to change or blame another, I can only change myself.
To let go is not to care for, but to care about.
To let go is not to fix everything, but to be supportive.
To let go is not to be protective, it is to permit another to face reality of the real world.
To let go is not to deny but to accept.
To let go is not to nag, scold, or argue, but to search out my own shortcomings and take self-inventory and correct them.
To let go is not to criticize and regulate, but to try to become what I dream I can be.
To let go is not to regret the past, but to grow from the past and live for the future.
To let go is to fear less and give love more.

Let Go and Let God

God, You Have Failed Me

Just ask yourself, "Why am I back here? Why am I back in jail? Why have things gone wrong for me? I used to read the Bible, go to church, and pray. But where did it get me? I'm still doing time. God failed me. But did he? I got in trouble. Did God tell me to break the law? While I was attending church and praying, did I act on what I read, or did I just go through the motions?" Then I realized that anyone can read directions to go through the motions; anyone can read directions to fix something that is broken, but if you don't fix it as the directions say, you will never fix it correctly.

If you lived like the Bible, Jesus says you would not have broken the law. I see so many inmates come to church, wear the cross, sing in the choir, read the Bible, even quote their favorite Bible verses, and pray before meals. These are all great starts to the road of eternal life with Jesus, but you cannot go halfway; you must go all the way. When you're swearing with girls or lust after them, how can you say, "God, how can you fail me?" Who really failed? Who wore his cross, read his diary, and spoke with him daily? Yet you would not trust him enough to walk with him toward the light. What you don't realize is he is still here for you, and his arms are always there to hold you no matter what crime you have done.

Many people believe that because they have discovered Jesus, he will be a great bail bondsman or parole god. But that isn't how it works. It is true: God does work in mysterious ways, but he will not step in and change what crimes and sins you have already committed. He will only bring you peace and love and will be there by your side always. No prison walls, no stone or steel or cement wall can stop him from being with you. He is always there for you, Jesus meets us where we are. He doesn't stand at the finish line and say, "I'll meet you here." Instead he comes alongside us and says, "I am with you always. I am with you on the good days. I am with you on the bad days. I am with you when you succeed. I am with you when you fail. I will see you through and we will cross the finish line of victory together." But you cannot see him until you open your eyes and heart. From that moment on, he will be with you one hundred percent, but you must also be with him one hundred percent. God knows that man has his faults, and he also knows if you are truly trying to be with him or just going through the motions.

Remember, if you have broken the law and sinned, then you must still be judged by your brothers and sisters. But God will do your time with you, and when you are released, if you follow his guiding light, you will never again say, "God has failed me!" because God never fails us. If you follow his teaching, you will have life abundantly; but you must also admit your sins, repent, and pray for forgiveness and really try not to ever do those sins again.

Do not think God is a fool. People go out, shoot, and rob someone time after time; before and after each robbery, they go and buy drugs and feel no remorse. But now they are dying; they want to repent. God knows that this is not repentance from the heart. This is fear, fear of God's judgment, and you should feel fear at that point.

Many people may say, "But what if there isn't a God, and when you die, that's it?" That's a good point, except what if there is a God and you have not asked for forgiveness? You must be judged for your life here on earth. Let's say, because there is a God, we must have Satan. Do you know what life with Satan would be like? Let me give a hint. How about those building fires where people would rather jump out of a ten-story building to their death than burn? That is real fear! So now you know what living for eternity with Satan would be like. You would be burning like that forever. And once you are there, it's too late to repent. You won't know fear until that day. So would you rather repent now on earth and lead a happier and blessed life so when your time comes, you can live with God in heaven for eternity? Or take the chance, turn your back on God, and when your party life of sin is over (which may only have lasted, say, eighty years), be judged and sent; be one of Satan's tortured souls and burn in fire forever. I know I am scared and want to let God know that I want to be with him, and that I am asking for forgiveness for all my sins each and every day. I know because I accept God into my life and allow him to lead me to his light. I will avoid many unhappy moments and help myself from returning back to prison.

Now, do not think that life will be perfect. Life is also a test, and God wants to always test you to see how faithful you are. Of course, he could have put you on earth, say on a road with all the bad things fenced off, where no one could see (you) them or touch (you) them. Then, at the end of the road, God would say you have all done well. So you must all love him, and each of you will have eternal life. But Jesus said, "Let's remove the fences and give (you) them the chance to prove how much they love God." That way only the ones who truly love him will have eternal life. Yet Jesus said, "Let me be the one chance to return home if they stray off the path." So Jesus gave his life that we may repent and ask for forgiveness. He is our one chance, the only way to return home to our Father.

So we can live on earth as we like, but remember, we've been warned of future danger and shown the way to be saved. It is up to you to grab hold of the lifeline and hold on for eternal life, and maybe you will never have to blame God that he failed you.

To My Sister with Love

My life has been through a stormy night's rain.

While sleeping last night, I had a dream; it left a tale to tell: I saw an angel; she wasn't looking well. Her body was bruised and battered, her wings ripped and torn. I saw that she could barely walk. She was tired and she was worn. I walked over then and asked her, "Angel, how can this be?" She tried to smile as she gathered her thoughts; then these words she said to me, "I am your guardian angel. Quite a task as you can see. You have lived a very wild life, with that you must agree. You have broken the law and broken hearts; you see what you have done to me. These bruises are from shielding you. I do my best even still. The drugs you have used so dangerously, I often pay the bill. My wings you see are ripped and torn, a noble badge I bare. So many times they have shielded you from dangers that you were unaware. Yes, each mark bares a story of pain and dangers I have destroyed. You made me wish, more than once, that I was unemployed. If you would only embrace life and choose to do so on your own, it would stop the pain and suffering that comes from being alone. I will always be there to watch over you, until my powers fail." When I awoke, I thought about the dream, how much for life I care. Then I looked around my prison cell, and my heart sank in despair. As for helping myself from within these walls, I wonder, *Should I even try?* Then distantly I could hear an old frail angel cry.

"Sincerely, your guardian angel." You are my angel from God.

Stopping the Generational Curse Cycle

Many families are unaware that they are caught up in generational curses because it is so normal and natural to them. It's not until they get counseling or they really look at the outside world that they see their world is warped and wicked and sometimes twisted.

Certain behaviors are learned just by watching others. It's called vicarious reinforcement. It doesn't have to be, for example, in direct exposure to a vicious dog to develop phobia. If I witness someone else experience that situation, that can have an impact on me, and I can develop a phobia.

I had an uncle that fondled his stepdaughter ever since she was a small child; she could remember being touched and fondled. It wasn't until she became pregnant with a child that she discovered that some of her cousins had experienced the same, yet no one ever discussed it.

She struggled with seeking help or remaining silent for fear of tarnishing the family's reputation.

When she became a mother, she could no longer keep her family's dirty little secret. She broke her silence and left home and left the child there to be raised by the parents. Although she needed counseling, but never received it by the family.

Most families have them, and they can be broken. A generational curse is defined as "family bondage" passed down from one generation to the next. Many families are unaware that they are caught up in generational curses because it is so normal and natural to them.

It's not until they decide to get counseling or they really look at the outside world that they see their world is warped and wicked and sometimes twisted.

Negative patterns of behavior that could be considered generational curses are physical abuse, sexual abuse, substance abuse, and alcoholism. It's a problem that has the family bound up, whether it's teen pregnancy and Grandmamma was a teen momma and Momma was one and you're one and you never married the father. That's the family being bound up in a very negative situation. And it seems natural and normal, hoping that you married the child's father. I had to experience this situation with my two children's fathers. It was painful.

Divorce could also be considered a generational curse. People whose parents had multiple divorces and then they have multiple divorces.

People imitate what they see, which oftentimes makes a generational curse a "learned behavior." I think one generation may fall into a bad habit or negative situation, and they were never able to pull themselves out of it, and they wind up making it internalized into the family system, and the ones that follow them just follow that pattern. The generational curse is a cycle that reflects a pattern that's been going on for years of "disconnection, disaffection and dysfunction."

It's a trans-generational perpetuation of a pattern of behavior that has an oppressive grip on a sizable proportion of our African American community. Negative patterns of behavior that are perpetuated are often taught.

Certain behaviors are learned just by watching others. It's called vicarious reinforcement. I don't have to be, for example, in direct exposure to a vicious dog to develop a phobia.

Childhood is a crucial period in shaping a child. I believe that it is important for every child to have at least one positive adult in his or her life who adores them.

That person provides a reflection of us as a worthwhile and lovable person. When that occurs, then an individual has the freedom to explore different ways of thinking, feeling, behaving, viewing themselves, and viewing others.

If that mirror is distorted, then that person is likely to develop a negative image of himself. So many of our kids—because of the parents of these kids—are operating with distorted, cracked, fragmented mirrors.

It's very difficult for them to reflect a positive view of the child. A generational curse can be put to an end. Breaking generational curses to begin a healing process for your family involves the following steps:

Usually deep inside of us, God puts a little warning signal that calls discernment that tells us something is not right. You have to start listening to yourself and believing yourself and valuing yourself enough to hear the warning that your inner self is giving you.

Once you face that situation, tell somebody and talk about it. Talk to your pastor, your counselor, or friend. By talking to somebody, that helps you to get some light on your situation to see whether it's normal or not.

Seek early intervention. This is the key before the anger and bitterness provides it a fertile ground. When the heart hardens and defenses become rigid and trusting others becomes difficult, hope and optimism begin to fade. So intervening at a very, very early age is important. Know that you have power over your life. We don't have to keep on being victims. It's been said that the first time you're a victim. The second time you're a volunteer when you see the situation coming, and you let it happen again. Be bold enough to call a wrong a wrong. That means that you have to have the power and believe in God that you can stand up and maybe tell your family members the situation has to stop. It takes a lot of guts to be able to do that.

Cut the connection and move on with your life. Be brave enough to step out of that situation. If you are going to break that curse, it might mean that you are not able to hang out with these friends or family members anymore. We've got to remember that family systems can be very strong, so pulling away to save yourself may be painful, but it may be your only way out. Convey hope that there is the possibility of change. There is the possibility that the way things have been doesn't necessarily reflect that it is the way things will always be. We have to change our pattern of behaving. The best predictor of future behavior in the absence of a powerful change agent intervening is past behavior. So something has to change. We know that unless a major intervention occurs and quickly. What we're likely to see in future generations would be of nightmarish proportion.

Stop keeping secrets. If we are *true* with ourselves, *we will admit that* a lot of us, most of us have some type of family mess, and it's been going on for more than one generation if we're honest about it, but we're so easy to point a finger. But the big deal is people keep secrets in families a lot. So the stuff you and I are going through now, Momma might be too embarrassed to say, "Well, that same thing happened to me." But if your parents would open their mouths and kind of talk about what they went through, that will show us a pattern that maybe we, the enlightened generation, can do something about. Silence really keeps evil going on in our household, so I encourage you to invite God in and break that generational curse cycle, so that your children and their children's children can have a better life. The generational curse has been broken off my seed and my life.

When Our Dreams Are Shattered

We begin with Joseph as a teenager. God began to deal with Joseph when he was only seventeen. Not everything that Joseph did was good. We are told that he brought to his father, probably regularly, an evil report of his brothers. There is nothing we can say here to make Joseph look good. This just added to his father's sorrow, and it got his brothers into trouble. Nobody likes a tattletale, so this only made his brothers angry and caused jealousy. Two things make a person a tattletale: their self-righteousness and their pursuit of self-vindication.

Joseph was self-righteous. We should be encouraged to learn that God can use a self-righteous person, for by nature we are like Joseph. We might have thought the writer would leave out his part of this story. Joseph is, after all, one of the heroes of the Bible. But the book of Genesis tell us that Joseph brought to his father the evil report because the Bible reveals the good and the bad about it's heroes. It is so encouraging to know that we do not have to be perfect to be wonderfully used by God.

Joseph was his father's favorite child. This could have had some advantages, but probably was more detrimental. It was most certainly not a very good thing at first, and Joseph suffered much because of it. Being the favorite of our parents might tend to give us self-confidence, but it also alienates us from our contemporary. Joseph had some personality and relationship problems. He was going to be used by God, yes, but he was not ready, just like so many of us, though we probably could not have told him that since he thought otherwise.

Do we want to be used by God? Are we quite sure we are ready to be used by the Lord? God knows whether we are. In the case of our lives and Joseph's, there was much sorting out in personality that had to be done, and I can tell you this: God can do it. God, as he prepares us to do his work, will sort out our personality defects, and we all have them.

As he prepares us to do his work, it is easy for us to say, "I am like this because my mother was this way," or "My father did this or that." It is easy to blame our parents for the way we are and the things that go wrong in our lives, and it's very wrong. We may be shy. We may be forward. We may be reserved.

We may be arrogant. But we should never think that any personality trait or hang-up or other blemish rule us out as God's messengers to our generation, for God can deal with us. He certainly dealt with me and Joseph and may others that suffered. A sovereign God shortly purged all the happy trimmings that accompanied Joseph's favored life.

We must remember that parents have their faults too. The reason that Joseph was the favorite child was partly because he was the son of Jacob's old age, but that does not excuse Jacob. However, we must forgive our parents and then hope that our children will forgive us. Nothing is more ridiculous than being bitter at our parents all our lives. We must sort ourselves out and let God deal with us until we take the responsibility for being just like we are.

Old Jacob, in order to show how much he loved Joseph, did what he thought was a good thing. He made Joseph a coat of many colors, "a richly ornamented robe" (Gn 37:3, NKJ). But Jacob did Joseph no favor in doing this. Worse than making it, though, was wearing it. Perhaps Joseph should have gone to his father and fallen down before him and said, "Please don't make me wear this." But Joseph was quite happy to put it on. He was a spoiled, arrogant teenager who was utterly insensitive to his brothers' feelings. When his brothers saw that his father loved him the most, "they hated him, and could not speak peaceably unto him" (Gn 37:4); that was a predictable reaction, and Jacob should have thought of that. It did not mean they hated their father—they hated Joseph. Jacob did this to the son that he loved so much, turning his other sons against Joseph. This is another caution for parents that it is harmful to show any kind of favoritism to a particular child. We are doing the child no favor at all. We are not even thinking of the child but only of ourselves. Joseph's coat of many colors did more for his father Jacob than it did for Joseph. Being partial is not a sign of love but a demonstration of our own weakness, which we are also passing on to a child.

The future governor of Egypt and God's man to preserve the seed of Abraham was off to a bad start. Perhaps we feel we had a bad break, with poor psychological or sociological beginnings. Maybe our parents are divorced or on drugs and a mental abuse. Perhaps we can look back on our childhood and say, "I have never had a good break." All we have seen about Joseph so far was a blueprint that spelled trouble for the rest of his life.

But there was also something at work in Joseph's life that was wonderful and positive, a gift that God gave him, just as God has given to each of us. One of the keys to understanding Joseph is provided by Stephen in Acts 7:9, "God was with him." If God is with us, there is no impediment, no personality difficulty, or nothing about class or background that can stand in the way of him making us a mighty instrument for our day. God was with Joseph, and he had a gift that would shape his own life and also the lives of others. God gave him dreams, which may not sound very impressive. Whoever would have thought a gift like that could mean so much? God has given to you something that nobody else can do because God made you different.

It is sometimes said of a particular person, "When God made so-and-so, he threw away the mold." But wait, he threw the mold away when he made us! We are all different from anybody else. Affirming the gift that God has given us is a way of glorifying our creator. Subsequent events in Joseph's life would reveal that this gift, this dreaming, which apparently included an ability to interpret dreams, saved his own life and the lives of his family.

But Joseph made a mistake. He told his dream to his brothers, and they hated him; we as people today have various gifts that God has given unto us, but our mouths get us into trouble and cause our loved ones to be jealous of blessings. He got them together when they could not do anything but listen to him and said, "Hear, I pray you, this dream which I have dreamed: for behold, we were binding sheaves in the field, and, lo my sheaf arose, and also stood upright; and behold, your sheaves stood round about, and made obeisance to my sheaf" (Gn 37:6-7). It was not very kind or clever to tell a dream like that. What Joseph did was what Jesus called "casting stones before swine" (Mt 7:6).

It is possible to abuse the gifts God has given us. It has sometimes been said that a man's genius is also his downfall. And Joseph, by abusing this gift, was alienating his brothers all the more. At this stage Joseph had now made three mistakes. First, he was a tattletale. Second, he flaunted his coat of many colors. Third, he abused the gift God gave him. Joseph should have kept the contents of his dream to himself.

Maybe God has revealed something to us, but we have a selfish need to tell it. We should ask ourselves why we want to tell it. Is it to make people admire us? God will exalt us in due time and when it's our season. We do not have to tell anybody! Remember this: if we have made a mistake, and God has not really shown us something, we will be very glad we kept quiet about it. It will save us from being embarrassed later. Keep in mind that Paul said, "Whether there be prophecies, they shall fail (1 Cor 13:8). If God has revealed something to us and we tell it around indiscriminately, I predict that we may wait a long, long time to be vindicated.

The fact that we have a gift from God does not guarantee we will have the wisdom or common sense to use it. Joseph told the dream, and it did not take any "dream expert" to give the interpretation. Joseph's brothers got the message like a flash. They said, "Shalt thou indeed reign over us? Or shalt thou indeed have dominion over us?" (Gn 37:8). They hated him more than ever. It did not do his brothers a bit of good to be told this dream. Flaunting a gift springs from a desire to be admired. But the result is always the opposite: it makes people positively dislike us.

Joseph was not ready just like so many of us to be used by God. His gift was in good shape, but he was not. Many of us may think we are right and ready because the gift is in operation. But God knows better. God had a plan for your life and for Joseph and for his people.

Giving ourselves completely to God, we may say, "If I give myself to God, my gift will never be known." I promise you, the only way our gift can be of value is for it to be sanctified and in the hands of our Creator and Redeemer. When we give our lives utterly to God, even be tempted in the end to say, "That's the way I was supposed to do it." This is that wonderful truth found in Romans 8:28, which says, "All things work together for good." The most stupid thing we have done turn out right. God does that!

What Joseph needed and so many of us as well was preparation and polishing: "We must through much tribulation enter into the Kingdom of God" (Acts 14:22). "The God of all grace, who called you to his eternal glory in Christ, will himself perfect, confirm, strengthen, and establish you" (1 Pt 5:10). "The Lord will perfect that which concerneth me" (Ps 138:8). This way will require some kind of suffering. God takes the big block we give him. He begins to chip away anything that is not just like his son. We have been predestined "to be conformed to the image of his son" (Rom 8:29). The day will eventually come when he can begin to use us. We might have thought Joseph would have surely learned by now to keep his mouth shut, something that God has to continue to work with us on in order to reach our destiny. Joseph was getting into all kinds of trouble. He should have learned that by telling his brothers his dreams he was making matters worse. But what do we read? He dreamed yet another dream and told it to them. Why hadn't he learned? The answer is that he had not been truly chastened yet. The reason God lets us suffer is to chip away what is not like Jesus in our lives, otherwise we will keep on making the same old mistakes. We may say, "Why do I do that all the time?" Perhaps it is because we have not yet submitted ourselves to God's refining fires. This is why James said, "Count it all joy when ye fall into diverse temptations" (James 1:2). May I suggest this? The next time a trial comes, rather than battle it out or try to get rid of it or grumble the whole time, accept it graciously. See what God does. Otherwise, eventually we will have to suffer what is almost unbearable because nothing else will work. God has to do that with us. He has had to do it with me. When I look back on my life, it is my suffering that I cherish most—not the blessing, not the bouquets, not the compliments, but my suffering. I don't wrestle with God at all because it is a fixed fight. The battle has already been won by God. God sees all things, and he knows all things. The battle is not yours, it's the Lord's. "The gifts and calling of God are without repentance" (Rom 11:29). That means that they are irrevocable. God gives us a gift, and we can keep using it because he does not take it away. Yet the continued use of a gift does not imply that everything else about us is right. The gift God gives us is like the salvation he gives us. He does not take it away—it is irrevocable. So here's Joseph—the gift is in operation, and he's repeating the same old mistakes, like so many of us do today. He was really getting carried away. Not only did he tell his second dream to his brothers, he also told his father. His father rebuked him, "Shall I and thy mother and thy brethren indeed come to bow down ourselves to thee to the earth?" (Gn 37:10). Although Joseph went too far by revealing great things to those who could not handle them, it is still obvious that God's spirit was at work. It is too easy to say that, unless everything goes exactly right, God is not in it. Joseph went too far, but who can deny that an authentic work was sent in operation in him? Joseph did not anticipate he would offend his father. When Joseph told his dream, he thought his father was going to like it. He thought his father would clap his hands and say, "Well done, Joseph."

Joseph was beginning the process of being emancipated from his father. Jesus said, "A man's foes shall be they of his own household. He that loveth father or mother more than me is not worthy of me: and he that loveth son or daughter more than me is not worthy of me" (Mt 10:36-37). Speaking personally, I too had to be set free from my children. I have already referred to my children, and thank God for them, but the time came when I had to break from them when I came behind prison walls. It happened many years go with my daughter, and at the time, I had to leave her in the care of my oldest sister, but it was a great trial for me. The Lord showed me certain things in the Bible, and when I came home to share the Lord with them, my son was happy about the Lord, but I thought she would be glad or clap her hands and say, "Oh, Mom, that's wonderful." But the opposite was the case, and it was not until recently that I won my daughter over. She now sees that God was using me, and it was no joke.

That, in part, is what was going on in Joseph's life. Jacob, the doting father, had manipulated Joseph. Joseph was now having to show he would not be completely controlled by his father. It wasn't pleasant for Joseph to be rebuked over what he thought would please his father. But then we read one other thing in this connection. Although Jacob rebuked him, Jacob "observed the saying" (Gn 37:11). The New International Version puts it, "His father kept the matter in mind." That means Jacob somehow knew in his heart that there was indeed something to Joseph's dream.

Jacob loved Joseph, and God love his son. But God loves his son perfectly and with a love with which we too are loved: "God so loved the world, that he gave his only begotten Son, that whosoever believeth in him should not perish, but have everlasting Life" (Jn 3:16). Joseph was a product of his father, and Jesus was a product of his Father, and our children are products of their seed (mother and father).

We are told that Jacob gave Joseph a robe of many colors. God wants to give us a robe of righteousness, the righteousness of Jesus Christ. On the cross, he was smitten of God. Not just rebuked, but smitten—put to death. All our sins were charged to Jesus. God punished Jesus instead of us so that we might be made in the righteousness of God in him.

It may be a good while indeed before God's greater purpose in us will be realized. It could be that you too are in a similar situation. Perhaps you are older, and you have yet to see what God's greater purpose in your life is. Perhaps you have just given up. Perhaps you are behind prison walls, and you are feeling all alone because loved ones have not visited you behind prison walls. Perhaps you are not receiving any mail from friends and family. You thought at one time that God was going to use you. You were convinced of it, but it did not work out. God's message to you right now is the end is not yet. The story—your life—is not over. Help is on the way, so stop wrestling with God, and let God mold and shape you to be the woman or mother and leader that he has called you to be in him. Behind prison walls was not an accident; it was ordained by God. God is right there with you.

STONES CAN'T STOP US

(Matthew 27:62-66 & Matthew 28:1-2)

I want you to take a look at verse 66: "sealing a stone, and setting a watch" and in verse 2, "the angel came and rolled back the stone from the door and sat on it." God is saying so much in my spirit behind prison walls. He sent me there, and he started to produce messages because of my afflictions. Death hit Jesus on Thursday evening, but then the grave held him through the weekend and tried to restrict him from getting up. When he rises from the dead, he looks back and said, "Death, where is your sting, and, Grave, where is your victory?" Some kind of way we have smashed the situation together and thought that they were the same thing, but they are two different distinctive enemies that come up against us to destroy us, limit us and binds us. On one hand he begins to minister about death which attached him swiftly. He submitted himself and became obedient unto death until he died more rapidly than the sinners which he was surrounded by. For they resisted death and struggled with it, but Jesus knew that death had its purpose in his life. He submitted to death and became obedient unto it, so much so, that when they came to him he was the first man dead they came for and they did not have to break his legs just as they did the other men who would have lifted there weight up off the cross and struggled against the death. He became obedient to death when they got to him. He was already dead and submitted unto him which fulfilled the scripture that said no bones in his body were to be broken and instead of breaking his bones they pierced him in his side and I thank God that they did because I was to be grafted in and I needed a place to be fixed too. You can't be grafted until there is a cut place and they cut him. (I'm still talking about Jesus now so stay with me readers), so that the body of Christ, may be engrafted and he became obedient until death and even the death of the cross. They put him in a barrow grave and left him there thinking that it was all over, the religious people were trying to destroy him and even after he was dead they were trying to make sure that he didn't get up again. The greater the power is, the greater the artillery that comes up against you. There is an equation between your potential and your attacks, and the enemy would not bother to send a machine gun out for a baby Christ. Because he knows how easy he could uproot a baby Christ with a mood swing when someone didn't speak to me, but when you graduate, he raises the artillery according to the age of the enemy and the ability of the person that he is going to attack. The greater the attack, the greater the anointing on your life will be. The greater the anointing, the greater the attack, and you must understand that before you start to, pray for it: "Lord, pour it on me and saturate me and use me. Set me aside and set me up and put me on exhibition." Because as you do that, the attack becomes more severe because the enemy was intimidated of the anointing that was on Christ. He began to send special security to make sure they keep him down. They put him in the grave, but then they rolled the stone over the top of the grave, and the stone represented those things that man puts in front of you to limit you, to stay in this perimeter and stay in this box you are in. "OK, but we want to make sure that you don't move beyond this perimeter and block you in, but its something that you need to understand, and that is that." They roll the stone, and they increase the security. This is what they said when they came to him, "and they said, 'sir we remember that the deceiver said while he was alive and after three days, he will arise again," and the sepulcher said: V-64.'"

They got a dead man, and they are worried that he would be greater then in death than he was alive. You see, Jesus has spoken so much in life that they were more afraid that they were going to be a movement that progresses and continues to flow, so they put guards around him, and they said, "We got to increase security on this dead man," and it's a twofold dilemma: they spoke about *(1) people they were afraid of who were going to get him* out *and* (2) *wanting* less men *to* get in. They assigned extra watchmen soldiers. This has nothing to do with death because he already died. This has to do with holding him where he is supposed to be, trying to keep him disconnected from his ministry and from what he is called here to do. So they went and made the sepulcher secure: sealing the stone and setting a watch; and when they sealed the stone, not only did they put a Roman seal on it, but also if you broke the seal, you had to face death from the king. So if any man would come along and overcome the guard and he sees the King's seal on it, he would not break the seal to go in and get Jesus out. One of these things that you need to understand in your life and ministry is with your walk with God and what you are doing. The enemy knows when there is great potential in your life; it may not have been realized. But if he knows that Jesus's mark is on you, if you ever get up, you will destroy him; if you ever get your life committed to God, you are going to be forced against him. So his strength is to watch to make sure that you never get out from behind the stone. He wants to keep you in a state of deadness and separation because he knows, if you ever get up, all that power and all that persistence and that strength will be used to tear Satan's kingdom down. Are you understanding what I am saying? You have to understand the fight before you can talk about the victory. You need to understand the conflict and the warfare; and you need to understand when there is great potential in your life, my life, or anybody's life. You need to understand that Satan strengthens the watch, the security, and that's why, as you mature in God, the battle becomes more intense. Because his strength is in the watch and that is why there are people who are strongly endowed who embark on sin, and when they get saved, God takes them and uses them mightily in the kingdom. And you ask God, How could you take somebody who I know so much about and use them so mightily? but Satan knew before they got saved that God wanted to use them. So he strengthened the watch to make sure that they stay in the grave because he knows, if they ever get loose, he is going to be in trouble. But why did he strengthen the watch? One thing was to destroy faith; he wanted a stone on him so tight that there will be sense of hopelessness because anytime that we wrestle with something bigger than us, that's blocking us, and that's intimidating us, the first temptation is to feel a sense of hopelessness. "I don't believe that Jesus is going to get up, but if he does get up, I want him to be so locked up behind that he just can't get out, and this is just extra insurance to security—to make sure that he stays in his place. I don't believe nobody is going to come here to get him out the grave; but if they do, I want them to be so intimidated of attacking the stone that I sent against him that, when they see the king's seal, those that would help him will back up and say "I'm not going in." So(1) there is a sense of trying to destroy the faith and (2) he wants no further activity. So that you are completely helpless and broken down, Satan will use any kind of stumbling block to stop you. He will use your health when you are just about to do something for God; and now your body begins to act up because he does not want no further activity. Just when you have made a commitment to the Lord, when you say, "Lord I am going to start bringing people to church," that's when your car breaks down because Satan has rolled a stone in front of you and he wants no further activity. Just when you are about to recommit your life back to God and you start to do what God has you to do, you lose your job and then you go into depression because Satan has rolled a stone in front of your life because he wants no further activity. And he wants to render you helpless and empty and wants you to go back into a cage of depression and be quiet and feel sorry for yourself because he is afraid that you may get loose. What they didn't mind was disciples worshipping where Jesus was, but they just did not want any new miracles. And the enemy does not mind dead religious; he does not mind worship of what used to be; he does not mind what Jesus used to do; he does not mind you coming to the tomb to bring frankincense and myrrh; he does not mind you talking about what Jesus did one time in your life; he does not mind you going to church except make sure nothing happens when you get there; he does not mind you giving money as long as you don't believe God will turn around your finances with the money that you give; he does not mind you singing in the choir or getting on the usher board, but as long as nothing change in your heart; he does not mind what's happening on the outside of you because Satan is not afraid of dead religions. He did not care how many people build shrines and monuments to what Jesus used to be. All he's done is put a stone between death and light because he does not want you to cross over into a real experience with God. Satan does not mind if you go to church as long church don't come to you, do you hear me? He does not mind if you dress up and coming out on Sunday morning, rocking a little and making fun of who's shouting, laughing, giggling, and going back home, shopping, having dinner, and saying, "OK, we paid God our bill." You see, Satan does not mind dead religions, and he is not concerned about that because he has not put a guard around dead religions and he does not mind you coming to the tomb. He just doesn't want you to go through the tomb. Are you hearing me? The purpose of the stone was (3) to stop his support; it would make a better message to say they did so he could not get out, but they had no idea that he would really get up. They really did it so no one could get in to him (I'm talking about Jesus). What Satan would do when you are going through a test is he will isolate you from any help—family, friends—because, when a stone is rolled in front of you, you begin to feel lonely; you feel like you don't have no help at all and like nobody is coming to see you and nobody cares. He wants to roll a stone away from you so that he can divide and conquer and set you all by yourself, but instead of sitting all by yourself, I want you to understand that God is not going to allow you to sit by yourself. What God is going to do is send a setup. You will not be set off; it is going to be a setup. And just when the enemy gets you set off on a stone in front of you and seals up the stone and gets you out of there by yourself, the setoff is going to be a setup. It's a setup for God to send divine intervention. God loves for you to put his children in a predicament where nobody can help them. He loves for you to put his children in a predicament where nobody can say I get the credit for bringing them out. God loves for you to be in a predicament where medicine is not working and the savings plans are not helping and nobody is calling and nobody is coming to see about you 'cause God does not intervene as long as people are doing fine. God only intervenes when man ceases to intervene. He only steps on the scene when people step off the scene. That's why you go through what you go through because sometimes people helping you will get in the way of God. Sometimes, you got to get all the way back in a corner where you have absolutely of no help. Paul said, "When my hour came to trial no man stood with me. Notwithstanding but the Lord stood with me." It's something about complete distraction that is a setup because the enemy begins to say, "I gotcha right where I want you at. I have tied up everything, and I rolled a stone in front of you, and even if you wake up, you can't get out because I got you locked up in, and I got a seal on the stone."

They buried Jesus and rolled a stone in front of Jesus and left him by himself, but what they didn't understand is that the help he needed was not on the outside—it was on the inside. You got to understand, when you got God in your life, if nobody comes to rescue you from the outside, you have enough power on the inside to take you through the storm. Inside, that's where you got to possess God, down on the inside, down on the innermost part of your spirit. You are going to need him on the inside so that's why you can't fool with vain religions because your religions cannot be tied up to a satchel and it cannot be tied up to candles and it cannot be tied to incense and it cannot be tied up to some system or any outside thing because, when you go through a storm, man won't be there; but down on the inside, they can't touch you. God wants to feed you if they put you in prison; you can have church at midnight. And if the put you in the fire, he will be the fourth one in the flame. You are not behind prison walls by yourself. What you got to have if you are going to live today and if you are going to do what God has called you to do today? If you are going to survive the times that we are now living in, you have to have divine intervention; and you cannot depend on the pity of people or circumstances or the economy or your job because, when you are in a faith fight, what can be shaken will be shaken so those things that cannot be shaken might remain. They messed up when they put a rock inside a rock and left a rock to hold a rock; and they didn't know that there was a rock behind a rock. And how can a rock stop a rock? But when you got Jesus down on the inside, somebody said that he's my rock of ages. Have you ever gone through a storm, and you didn't have nothing to hold on too but the rock on the inside of you, and you looked up and saw a rock in front of you, and when you looked in, you saw a rock inside of you? I'm so glad that there is a rock down on the inside of you, and when the storm is coming, you can use the rock in you to break the rock on the outside? Divine intervention. Divine intervention will increase your faith; it will put you in a state where you have got to believe God. Faith is never effective as long as you got a way out because you will always use the way out rather than believe God. The reason why we do not believe God for water is because we have it in the sink/bathrooms and we don't need water to come out of a rock—because water comes right out of the faucet/sink. But if you were in a desert and you couldn't get water out the faucet and when you're in a situation where you can't get it on your own, faith is made perfect when you are shut off by yourself. God has set you in a closed-up situation so that he can show you how strong he is because none of your normal tools are working. Stone can't stop us. I'm glad for every test because if it had not been for the Lord on my (your) side, where would I (you) be? You may be behind prison walls or you may be in prison within yourself, but the devil is scared of you; just continue to pray and praise God. I'm about to break out with my praise. I got up by the power of God; stones can't stop us. God will raise you up, so just hang on and hang in there because God is the only one you need because if God be for you, who can be against you?

God is going to make a stage out of the stone. They meant if for evil, but God is turning it for your good. It's just a stage; the stone is a stage. The greater the stone, the bigger the stage; your enemies would come to see you get stoned. You need to understand, if God has blessed you, who can curse you? "No weapon that is formed against you shall be able to prosper" (Isa. 54:17). God will work it out.

The first victory is when you wake up, and the second victory is when God brought you out. When Jesus woke up, he loosed himself, and Jesus folded up the dust napkin because he said, if he was coming out, he was coming out clean. God said if you lose something that he will give it back unto you, pressed down, and shaken together. God will give you double for your trouble. There ain't no stone in your face that you can't move. I am going through if I got to go by myself. Jesus will roll the stone away so that everybody can see where you used to be and that you are no longer there anymore. Stones, they don't stop us. I'm not going to break down; I'm learning how to glorify God while I'm going through. God will teach us how to survive the stones.

I went through hell behind prison walls because the devil was afraid that I would get up. I was told that I could not pray at work, and I work at the chapel. I was told that I could not pray at the unit that I lived in. The devil tried to set up a roadblock against me, and he tried to lock me in and put a box over me, but I cried out "Jesus," and Jesus told me that he was going to bring me out. They went out of their way to make me look bad, and you may be going through this right now. The more you do it, the more you win souls for Christ.

I was locked up, but I was not locked down spiritually. I was free because I learned that stones could not stop me because God delivered me from behind the prison walls. Stones can't stop God.

God will set you free. You are free in Jesus's name.

Amen.

Living In Troublesome Times

Let not your heart be troubled: Ye believe in God, believe also in me. In my Father's house are many mansions: if it were not so, I would have told you. And if I go and prepare a place for you, I will come again and receive you unto myself; that where I am, there ye may be also.
—John 14:1-3

According to the World Book Dictionary, *troublesome* means "giving trouble: causing annoyance; distressing." Yes, we are truly living in troublesome times if you just turn on the television and watch the evening news.

Trouble seems to be everywhere, but as Christians, we should not allow ourselves to be troubled by the things of this world. In John 16:33, Jesus says, "These things I have spoken unto you, that in me ye might have peace. In the world ye shall have tribulation; but be of good cheer, I have overcome the world." Hallelujah! Jesus has overcome the world. In Revelation 1:18, Jesus states, "I am he that liveth, and was dead; and behold, I am alive forevermore, Amen: and have the keys of hell and of death." Jesus triumphed over the devil. We serve a champion, and it took me to come to prison to realize all that I did not know about Jesus. Why then should we worry about the things of this world?

Psalms 46:1 states, "God is our refuge and strength, a very present help in trouble." We cannot lose with Jesus. First John 4:4 states, "Ye are of God, little children, and have overcome them: because greater is he that is in you than he that is in the world." Philippians 4:13 states, "I can do all things through Christ which strengtheneth me."

When trouble is around us, we have a tendency to fear, to be anxious, or to worry. But the Bible clearly says, "For God hath not given us a spirit of fear; but of power, and love, and of a sound mind" (2 Tm 1:17). Hebrews 13:5-6 states, "Let your conversation be without covetousness; and be content with such things as ye have: for he hath said, I will never leave thee, nor forsake thee. So that we may boldly say, the Lord is my helper, and I will not fear what man shall do to me." God will restore us.

Deuteronomy 31:16 states, "Be strong and be of good courage, fear not, nor be afraid of them: for the Lord thy God, he it is that doth go with thee; he will not fail thee, nor forsake thee." Sometimes we feel that God has forsaken us, and at times we feel that God is a million miles away and does not care about us, but this is a trick of the devil. God never leaves us; we leave God. We must come closer to God. James 4:7-8 states, "Submit yourselves therefore to God. Resist the devil, and he will flee from you. Draw nigh to God, and he will draw nigh unto you."

Apostle Paul says in 2 Corinthians 4:8-9 that "we are troubled on every side, yet not distressed; we are perplexed, but not in despair; persecuted, but not forsaken; cast down, but not destroyed." Why are we not distressed if we are troubled on every side? Because Jesus is our hope in the time of need and sorrow. Jesus will not fail us nor forsake us. Second Corinthians 4:17-18 explains the reason of Paul's optimism: "For our light affliction, which is but for a moment, worketh for us a far more exceeding and eternal weight of glory; while we look not at the things which are seen, but at the things which are not seen: for the things which are seen are temporal, but the things which are not seen are external." Paul was looking at the future toward his reward that would be in heaven! Did you catch this, "Light affliction, which is but for a moment?" We feel that we have a lot to go through on this earth. But Paul said our affliction is light. Well, think about it. Everything is light compared to what Jesus had to go through. Isaiah 53:3-5 states, "He is despised and rejected of men; a man of sorrows, and acquainted with grief: and we hid as it were our faces from him; he was despised, and esteemed him not. Surely he hath borne our griefs, and carried our sorrows: yet we did esteem him stricken, smitten of God, and afflicted. But he was wounded for our transgressions; he was bruised for our iniquities [sin]: the chastisement of our peace was upon him; and with his stripes we are healed."

Friend, I do not know what you are going through right now. You may have lost a loved one while being in prison, or you may be sick in your body. You may be suffering from a broken heat. Psalm 34:18 states, "The Lord is nigh unto them that are of broken heart; and saveth such as be of a contrite spirit." I want you to know that Jesus understands what you are going through, and he wants to give you peace, peace that passeth all understanding. Peace that man can not give you, but God. Do you want to have this peace that the Bible talks about? Philippians 4:6 states, "Be careful for nothing; but in everything by prayer and supplication with thanksgiving let your requests be made known unto God." Philippians 4:7 states, "And the peace of God, which passeth all understanding, shall keep your hearts and minds through Christ Jesus." What does this mean? It means pray to God. Tell God your troubles. First Peter 5:7 states "Casting all your cares upon him; for he careth for you." Matthew 11:28-30 states, "Come unto me, all ye that labor and are heavy laden, and I will give you rest. Take my yoke upon you, and learn of me; for I am meek and lowly in heart: and ye shall find rest unto your souls. For my yoke is easy, and my burden is light." Take just a minute and think about a friend or family member. Isn't it easy to talk to this person about your problem? It is because he or she seems to care and understand. Let Jesus be your friend; he will stick closer than a brother. He is a friend (Proverbs 18:24). John 15:13 states, "Greater love hath no man than this that a man lay down his life for his friends." Joshua 1:9 states, "Have not I commanded thee? Be strong and of good courage; be not afraid, neither be thou dismayed: for the Lord thy God is with thee whithersoever thou goest." Philippians 4:6 states, "Be careful for nothing; but in everything by prayer and supplication with thanksgiving let your request be made known unto God." Did you catch the word *thanksgiving*? Praise and thanksgiving gets our eyes off of the problem and turns our eyes upon the answer. We have always heard that we should pray, but do we ever hear that we should be thankful? Do you remember the story about Paul and Silas in prison? What were they doing? Grumbling or complaining? No, they were praising God. And what happened? They got out of prison. Acts 16:25 states, "And at midnight Paul and Silas prayed, and sang praises unto God: and the prisoners heard them." Verse 26 states, "And suddenly there was a great earthquake, so that foundation of the prison were shaken: and immediately all the doors were opened and everyone's bands were loosed." Being in prison mentally or physically is an experience of deliverance for God if you cry unto the Lord with a loud voice. Psalm 142:7 states, "Bring my soul out of prison, that I may praise thy name: the righteous shall compass me about; for thou shalt deal bountifully with me.

Isaiah 26:3 states, "Thou wilt keep him in perfect peace whose mind is stayed on thee: because he trusteth in thee." I ask a simple question, where do you put your trust: in man or in God? Man will let you down, but God will never let you down or disappoint you. You will have perfect peace if you keep your mind on Jesus because you will trust him. If you trust someone or something, you do not worry about it, right? Philippians 4:8 states, "Finally, brethren, whatsoever things are true, whatsoever things are honest, whatsoever things are just, whatsoever things are of good report; if there be any virtue and if there be any praise, think on these things." In verse 9, it continues, "Those things, which ye have both learned and received, and heard, and see in me, do: and the God of peace shall be with you." He is the God of peace. Isaiah 9:6 states, "For unto us a child is born, unto us a son is given: and the government shall be upon his shoulder: and his name shall be called Wonderful, Counselor, the mighty God, the everlasting Father, the Prince of Peace." You cannot be at peace if you are always concerning yourself with bad news now, can you? Bad news has a tendency to rub off on you and make you worry and feel bad.

John 16:33 states, "These things I have spoken unto you that in me ye might have peace. In the world ye shall have tribulation: but be of good cheer; I have overcome the world." Do you understand what this verse means? Many people have a misconception about salvation. They believe that if they go to church and live for Jesus, that they will not have any problems. Wrong! Jesus clearly states here that we will have problems, but we can overcome them because he has! John 14:27 states, "Peace I leave with you, my peace I give unto you: not as the world giveth, give I unto you. Let not your heart be troubled, neither let it be afraid." Jesus gives us our peace, but not like the world does. How does the world try to give us peace? The world tries to give us peace by offering us drugs and sex. Drugs and alcohol will calm our nerves, they say, and make us feel at ease for a moment. But my friend, when the drugs are gone, you are left more uneasy than when you were before. The world is quick to offer an easy solution, but today I offer you the word of God. Romans 6:23 states, "For the wages of sin is death; but the gift of God is eternal life through Jesus Christ our Lord." Hebrews 11:25 states, "Choosing rather to suffer affliction with people of God, than to enjoy the pleasures of sin for a season."

For friend, if you are searching for something to ease your pain and heartache, look to Jesus. He loves you. John 3:16 states, "For God so loved the world that he gave his only begotten Son, that whosoever believeth in him should not perish, but have everlasting life." John 3:17 states, "For God sent not his Son into the world to condemn the world; but that the world through him might be saved." We all sin; no one is perfect. Romans 3:23 states, "For all have sinned and come short of the glory of God." If you have not yet accepted Jesus Christ as your Savoir, do so today. You may never have another chance.

The Riches of God's Grace

It is a sure mark of grace to desire more. Being in the wilderness, your faith will be tried to see what you are made of.

Just like Shadrach, Meshach, and Abednego, we're all thrown into the fiery furnace. "And the king Nebuchadnezzar full of fury, and the form of his visage was changed against Shadrach, Meshach and Abednego: therefore he spoke, and commanded that they should heat the furnace once seven times more than it was wont to be heated." (Daniel 3:19)

There was a fourth body in the fiery furnace; they were not alone. God came before me on this journey. I came later to join Jesus. I could not have done this journey without the Lord by my side. I've had some good days, and I've had some bad days, but my good days outweigh my bad days. My faith was put in the fiery, the pulling, and the flesh dying every day.

I had to die to my flesh, and at times, I had to pray without ceasing. I had to stay on my face and pray. Why? Because God was getting me ready to birth the baby that he has placed inside of me. I came to prison to deliver my baby.

Being in the wilderness caused me to reflect on life. It also caused me to get a personal relationship with the Lord. I had to depend upon the Lord for everything, "my life . . . to keep me strong." "God is our refuge and strength, a very present help in trouble" (Ps 46:1).

God had to cleanse me, purge me, mold me, transform me, dying to the flesh in order to do his will and not mine own. God then began to make me over from being broken.

You will never know what you are made of if you have never been tested or broken.

I humble myself before the Lord. "The fear of the Lord is the instruction of wisdom and before honor is humility" (Pr 15:33).

There is a place where the devil can't find you if you abide in God's word. God began to deal with me during my wilderness. Something has happened to me; I have found a landing place in the Lord." Dying to your flesh daily is a process.

God rescued my soul by bringing me out like pure gold. And now I want the world to know. Being in the wilderness caused me to grow.

What if you received an invitation to a private reception at the largest gathering in town? What if, when you arrived, you learned the reception was in your honor because someone had placed in your name with inexhaustible?

How would you feel to know that regardless of what you did or how much you spent, your riches were limitless?

Do you know that God loves you so much that he's already deposited into your account unconditional and unending riches that are worth so much more than money? Did you know that riches of God's grace are not just indescribable blessings for our future but realities we can enjoy now in this lifetime? He has assured us that he will provide everything we need according to his unlimited resources (Philippians 4:9) and that he "is able to do far more abundantly beyond all that we ask or think" (Eph 3:20).

All the riches of his grace are bestowed by God alone—they can be given by no one else. Therefore, they also never will be taken away because, upon salvation, these riches are given to us through the merits of Jesus Christ. God bought me out. God bless you. Amen!

Real Commitment

I remember when I was in sales. I believed that the relationship does not end at the moment of the sale; that is when the relationship begins.

Transformation begins when we accept Jesus Christ as our personal Lord and Savior. This is when our journey of faith begins, not ends.

When we accept Christ as our Savoir, we develop spiritually and turn our lives over to a power greater than ours. Turning our lives over to him is the hard part of the journey of faith.

As Christians, we must avoid disputing and striving. We must look up to Christ and follow the examples he demonstrated for us by the life he led, and we must follow his teachings. You choose the person you are to be; if you are a mean person, you respond to meanness with further meanness. If you are a person of love, you respond to meanness with love. The Christian is commanded to be a person of love.

Jesus teaches valuable lessons, such as turning the other cheek. Many people try to teach such lessons to their children when they are unable to learn themselves. The best example of our Lord's teaching is Jesus Christ himself. When Jesus was being crucified, his character was that of love and compassion for the very people who were abusing him. Jesus said if someone wants to sue you and take your tunic, let him have your cloak as well. We Christians have a difficult time following this.

I know personally many stories of people who claim to be followers of Christ who have trouble following this teaching.

We live in a society that claims to be predominately Christian, but is manipulated by the judicial system where the first line of action is the courts.

If you are not following his teaching, you are not a Christian. You might call yourself a Christian, you might be present in the church, but you are really just a wannabe. You want to be a Christian, you call yourself a Christian, but you do not follow Christ.

A Christian is someone who not only accepts the gift of God but someone who takes action according to his commands.

If someone forces you to go one mile, go with him two miles. Wow! Go an extra mile with your oppressors. Shoot, we won't even walk to church anymore, much less be nice to our oppressors.

Jesus teaches us to give to the one who ask. Do we do it? Not really. Notice that Jesus didn't say give to only good people, give only to the good causes, or give only to the things you approve of.

As Christians, we must act according to Jesus. We must make a real commitment, not just say it, but do it. Jesus teaches us that we must be kind to all and to love your enemies and pray for those who abuse you. That's some real tough stuff there. It is hard enough for us to pray to begin with, much less to pray for our enemies

COMMITMENT AND RECOMMITMENT

Before coming to prison, I had already committed myself to the Lord, and when I arrived behind prison walls, I recommitted myself and my life to the Lord.

Many people are controlled and dominated by things like circumstances and fear and bitterness and unforgiveness and greed and a lust for their self-pleasure. These things are driving people through life. And I tell you, if you are going to be a person that makes a difference in life, you need to be driven by commitment. The quality of the difference you make will be totally determined by what you are committed to and your level of commitment.

Paul said in 2 Corinthians 5:14, "It is the love of Christ constraineth us that compels me." He said, "I am compelled, I am driven, by the love of Jesus Christ." This incredible commitment came because Paul realized that Jesus had committed himself to him and each of us. Now he is saying, "I am being driven today by that commitment that I have now made to Jesus." Here is the point: we as people need to be wise in what we choose to be committed to because our commitments will cause us to make poor choices in life and suffer with lifelong pain later in life. Our commitments determine the way we end up and how we become.

The key verse is 2 Chronicles 16:9. It says, "The eyes of the Lord searching the whole earth in order to strengthen those hearts are fully committed to him." The eyes of the Lord are searching. He is looking for people who he can support, who he can strengthen, who he can undergird. He is looking for a specific quality, and that is people whose hearts are committed fully to him. What does it mean to be fully committed to Jesus? In the words *fully committed,* there is the implication that there are different levels of commitment—partial commitment or casual commitment or half-hearted commitment—and let me elaborate a little bit because, you see, I was once one of those people that have been in the past that served Jesus half-heartedly until storms after storms came upon me where I just couldn't handle it on my own. I need Jesus in my life. I was one of the hardheaded that could not be told anything because I already knew every thing; well, I was wrong, and so are you, and some people are afraid to commit to Jesus because of partying and dancing. But you don't know what you are doing is changing partners so that you can have a better life. We go through life committed to someone or something, so if you don't commit yourself to the Lord, then you have committed yourself to the devil, and that is death. Dead does not mean "graveyard dead" but spiritually dead, and that's true. There are different levels of commitments.

God says though, "I am looking for people whose hearts are fully committed to me, and I will come and bring strength and support to their life."

Being behind prison walls is not easy on no one because I cried out to the Lord all the time. There were some people who could not understand because I had such a short journey, but the length of time did not matter. It was just the point that I was out of my comfort zone; and my husband, family, and church friends could not help me—nobody but God. I had to learn to depend on Jesus for everything, to take full care of me and to protect me. So God had to take me to his secret place of security: Psalm 91:1. I stood on that chapter the whole time that I was on my journey for the Lord because sometimes in life God has to hide us in order to birth out what he has birthed in us. Jesus had to teach me that I was not in control of "nothing." I had to develop an attitude of gratitude. I had to learn to appreciate the simple things of life and not take people places and things for granted. I began to realize that this journey was all about Jesus and not self. I cried at night many times after the lights were out, and people would always hear me sniffling and weeping to the lord because all I wanted to do is to please Jesus, so Jesus had to crucify my flesh each and every day.

I had to experience how other inmates would grin in your face and talk about you in your face, but what was the talk about? so who was I? Nobody compared to Jesus. Later on Jesus began to break them down one by one because he had already spoken to me and said, "My child, 'be still, and know that I am God: I will be exalted among the heathen'"; so I had to hold fast and let him fight my battles for me, and sometimes that meant just to keep me and my big mouth close." Take your mouth off of God's people, because his word says in Psalm 105:15, "Touch not mine anointed, and do my prophets no harm." We as people have cut our own blessings by cursing other people. Deuteronomy 28:1,6 speak on blessings and curses.

I had to fully commit myself to the Lord so that my whole family, my daughter, son, sisters, and brothers would be saved and filled with Jesus's Holy Spirit and pass the love of Jesus on to somebody else. You may be angry because you were molested at a young age by a family member; you may be angry with your parents because you didn't receive love; you may be angry with your husband or wife because they have been cheaters all during the marriage; you may be angry at yourself because of a generational curse of drugs and alcohol; you may be angry because the system has failed you, and loved ones are behind prison walls, but what don't kill you will make you stronger in the Lord and yourself. Everybody is not celebrating Jesus Christ on the same level. I want to say there is great grace in this. We are all in the process. I don't know that there is anybody, including myself that has perfected in any of the areas. We are still healing from some kind of hurt in our lives. But I believe this is what Jesus looks for when he talks about full commitment. And again, nothing really happens unless people are fully committed.

The first commitment is this, and it is foundational. It is the most important issue that you will ever settle in your heart. There is no other issue more important than that one.

Question: Is Jesus Christ who he says that he is?

Question: And am I going to be committed to him?

It is absolutely foundational. I believe people in our lives to think there are other sorts of commitments that need to be made that are maybe either just as important or more important than this one—for instance, the career decision, the career commitment. For example, we get out of school and realize that Mom and Dad aren't going to do the handout anymore and so the question we need to answer is what are we going to live on? This is an important issue that we need to figure out because this happened to me with my mother growing up; and I began to get upset and an angry feeling of extreme hostility toward my mother, but not realizing that I was eighteen years old and smelling myself, but not knowing that I would be a mother someday and what goes around will come back around to you with your very own children. Until I came in knowledge of the truth that my mother gave me life and that she didn't owe me a thing once I became an adult and that I owe it to the Lord and myself to be all that God has created me to be and then have forgiveness to place in my heart, her job was finished. Then there is this other issue that I think is also important, but it is one that I think oftentimes we elevate it so high, and that is the marriage issue. Who am I going to be married to or am I going to be single all my life? These two questions, what am I going to live on? and who will I share my life with? are certainly vital, but readers, can I tell you something? You can mess up on those two, and it will create all kinds of heartaches and pain and suffering, and it really hurts, but still these decisions don't have eternal consequences like these next ones do. Who am I going to live for? Who am I committed to?

Everybody is going to live for something, and I think it is vital to intentionally decide just who and what you will live for because that is what will drive our lives. When we decide that the primary commitment in our life, the foundational commitment in our life is Jesus Christ, I am telling you we step into the place where we can now make a difference in life.

God had to teach me how to lean on him and not man. God had to teach me how to wait on him for an answer. I hear the voice of the Lord saying that he will bring you out, but you have to come where the overflow is, and that means recommitment. It's time for you to make the devil mad. No matter what you are going through, God still deserves the praise and honor.

There are two things I think God really wants to build into us in terms of our commitment to him and that is, first, that we believe Jesus Christ is alive, that God raised him from the dead, and he is alive today. And also, that he is the Lord. When you begin to make a decision as to whether or not he is going to be the Lord, you always, in any commitment you make, you always need to look at two factors. First of all, you need to look at cost, and then you look at the benefit.

Anytime you make a commitment, there is always going to be a cost, always. But then there are also benefits. You need to look at the price tag and then the payoff. So what is the cost of making Jesus Christ the Lord? You give up control. You are not the boss anymore. You have to go to him and say, "Lord, what do you want me to do? I'm not calling the shots anymore, I'm yours. I have been resurrected with Christ." "And it is not me living anymore, but Christ living in me. And the life that I now live," Paul says in Colossians 2:22, "I live by faith in the Son of God who loves me and gave his life for me." He is the Lord. He is in control. He is making the decision, not me. I am not living for myself. I am not living for money. I am not living for pleasure. I am living to please Jesus because he is the Lord. There is great benefit when we come to a point of confessing that he is the Lord. The benefit is this: I know then I am forever fully forgiven of everything I have done wrong and will ever do wrong. I am completely forgiven. Then God says, "Not only that but I am going to empower you to live the kind of life that you want to live that blesses me and brings honor to my name." My friend, those are good benefits. But it starts with making him the head of your life. I think you need to settle that; you have to settle that is he the Lord? Is he in charge? Is he calling your shots? I guess it is not standard for you to call on his name wherever you are. But even if you have received Jesus in your heart as your personal savior, my question is, can you confess that he is God and God all by himself? He is God of my life. He is making decisions for me. He is guiding me and directing me. That is a foundation commitment that we make. He is God!

The second one is if you want to make a difference in life you commit to be a member of God's family. You commit to be a part of the family. First Peter 1:3 says, "God has given us privilege of being born again so that we are now members of God's own family." In God's great love for his people, he saw that we would need support, we would need perspective, we would need to have truths spoken to us in love, we need to be confronted at times, we would need prayer, we would need a helping hand in care; and so God said, "Look!" It all starts foundationally as you commit your life to Jesus Christ. But then there is the other step, and that is you enter into the privilege of being part of the family of God of being committed to that family. (Hello? Are you listening? I kind of feel like I am by myself. This will help me. Say, giddy up, my sisters, my brothers, go for it!) There are people in the world, and they are behind prison walls that's fighting for your life that we take for granted. We have the privilege of being part of the family of God. Martin Luther said, "God is our Father, but the church is our Mother." God is calling us not only to be committed to him but also to each other. I love this verse, Romans 12:10; it says, "Be devoted to one another." Be devoted to each other because that is why God made this, if we are ever going to ever make a difference. I thank God for the women; when my faith here a few months ago was beginning to waver and beginning to step back away from what I really knew was the will of God *because* I was so full of fear, there were some praying sisters that got around me and prayed me through and that *assured me* we are going to move forward in this thing, we are going to move forward in the Kingdom of God. I know that my husband was praying for me and also my church family, and that is why we need one another. We have this great privilege of being members of the body of Christ. I am committed to living my life as a servant of God. But I believe there needs to be commitment in our hearts to say, "I want to be like Jesus," and we as people have to grow in our ability to think like Jesus and then to care like Jesus and act like Jesus and to make decisions like Jesus and to treat people like Jesus. "My belief, my behavior, my attitudes, and my actions, all *are* coming out of a heart that says 'God loves me, therefore I love him. Therefore, I am going to live my life like Jesus lived it.'"

We are all in process. Wouldn't it be nice if we could take a Jesus pill because we take pills for everything else? Wouldn't that be awesome? I got a Jesus pill, sisters and brothers; I am there. It doesn't happen that way, but if I could just suggest something, that might promote the life of Jesus in your life.

Hebrews 6:1 says, "Let us go on . . . and become mature in our understanding, as strong saints ought to be." Proverbs 23:12 says, "Commit yourself to instruction; attune your ears to hear words of knowledge." The starting point of moving on into maturity is becoming the kind of people that God will use to make a difference in the lives of others; so take the Bible off the shelf out of your lockers, blow off the dust, open it up, and begin to absorb the attitudes and the desires and the heart of Almighty God. Let him transform your mind; be transformed by the renewing of your mind—take it in. I'm taking you deep inside because it was God who kept me when I could not keep myself, and if you are behind prison walls and if your stay is long or short, you are going to need him. And as you do, God says, "I will change you and your situation." That is the way change happens.

Here is the third thing: I must commit to be a minister of his grace. *A minister of his grace.* When I say that, I am not talking about becoming a pastor, so don't freak out. OK! I am not talking about being a pastor. Many are called, but few are chosen. Some of you may become a pastor. I don't know, when I say minister, what I am talking about here is that whenever you use your talents, your abilities, and the things that God has built into your life—your spiritual gifts, your affections, your abilities, your personality—you use all that to unselfishly help others without any sense of reward or remuneration. That is called ministry. When you care about people, when you want to help them, when you see them in need and you step into that need and bring them whatever you have, that is called ministry; and I want to tell you that every child of God is called to be a minister. Every one of us! We are called to be ministers. And when we step into that and commit to minister God's word, he will support us. So remember, if you want to make a difference in life, you must be committed to being a minister of his grace wherever God tells us to go.

Here is the fourth thing: commit to being a messenger of his love. *A messenger of his love.* Ultimately, I think this is one of the greatest things that will change the world. Second Corinthians 5:19 says, "For God was in Christ, restoring the world to himself." This is the wonderful message he has given to us to tell others. We are Christ's ambassadors. God is using us to speak to others. The moment you become a believer, you became an ambassador. God said, "I want you to take this ministry now that I am done with you, as I have reconciled you to myself, and I want you to tell other people about this." The best news I ever heard was when someone explained to me that Jesus Christ came to the earth, and when he died on the cross, he forever fully forgave me of all my sin.

Commitment is a powerful thing. If you cannot commit to God, then you cannot commit to a husband or wife—submit, commit, and recommit. Think about just how committed you are for a minute. It is a challenging thing to consider. It may be a bit hard to look at your life and see your commitment level, but let me tell you something. As important as it may be to consider that question, I think it is probably the wrong question to consider if you want to ramp up your commitment level.

Question: Do you know how committed the Lord is? I am telling you this great God in heaven is so mightily committed to you and me, and when you realize the depth of his commitment for you, it can only drive you into being committed to his heart and to his kingdom. God bless you.

Changing Your Way of Thinking with an Expecting End

Behind prison walls, I have experienced various women that had stinking thinking, and it's the same way with us. We have to conceive it on the inside in order to receive it and achieve it on the outside. If you don't think you can have something wonderful in life, then you never will. The barrier is in your head/mind. Your own wrong thinking can keep you from God's best for your life.

You too may have assumed that you'll never leave prison, or when you leave prison, that your life is over. But you are wrong; that is the stinking thinking: that you will never be more successful. *I'll never achieve the significance, do something meaningful with my life, or enjoy the finer things in life that I've seen others enjoy.*

Sad to say, you are exactly right, unless you are willing to change your way of thinking. Enlarging your vision because people without vision perish, and that means division.

To conceive it, you must have an image on the inside of the life you want to live on the outside. This image has to become a part of you in your thoughts, your conversation, deep down in your subconscious mind, in your actions, in every part of your being. It starts wherever you are because if you can't start in prison, then you can't wait until you get home to start because it starts in the mind in order for it to manifest down in your spirit.

What you keep before your eyes will affect you. You will produce what you're continually seeing in your mind. If it's your choice—defeat or failure—then you're going to live that kind of life. But if you develop an image of victory, success, health, abundance, joy, peace, and happiness, nothing on this earth will be able to hold those things from you. Not a devil in hell can't.

Too many times, bad situations strike our lives, and we find ourselves in a rut, thinking we've reached our limits. We don't really stretch our faith; we don't believe if we don't see it. Faith is the substance of things hoped for and the evidence of things unseen, so why believe what you can see? God wants to increase you financially, by giving you a job of your heart's desire and choice. Have you ever seen yourself accomplishing your dreams and reaching your goals? You must replace that vision in your mind that you can do all things through Christ who strengthens you and that you are above and not beneath; you are a lender and not a borrower. You must speak life into your situation and not death.

Being behind prison walls does not mean that your life is over; it is a new beginning. There are people that are not locked up behind prison walls, and they are in prison within themselves. Now that's prison.

It's important that you program your mind for success. That won't happen automatically. Each day, you must choose to live with an attitude of gratitude that expects good things to happen to you each day. The Bible says, "Set your mind and keep it set on the higher things." When you get up in the morning, the first thing you should do is set your mind on Jesus, and he will direct your day in the right direction. Speak life into your day and say, "This is the day that the Lord has made, and I will rejoice and be glad in it," and get excited about today! Start your day with faith, peace, and love and expectancy; and then go out anticipating something good. And good things will happen. Expect your circumstances to change in your favor. Expect people to go out of their way to help you. Expect to be at the right place at the right time.

God usually meets us at our level of expectancy. If you don't develop the habit of expecting good things to come your way, then you're not likely to receive anything good. If you don't expect your marriage to get better or whatever you are dealing with to get better, they probably won't. Our expectations set the boundaries for our lives. Jesus said, "According to your faith . . . be it done to you."

Some people tend to expect the worst, and they have no faith at all working in their life. They go around with that poor-old-me mentality, always negative. Well, why not you? Always depressed. "God, why don't you do something about my situation?" Other people honestly feel so overwhelmed by their troubles they have difficulty believing that anything wonderful could happen to them. "Oh, I've got so many problems. My marriage is in trouble. My children won't do what's right. My business isn't doing well, my health is going bad. I had a setback for a greater comeback." Friend, that's what faith is all about and that's how God works in our lives. Are you expecting to experience the goodness of God, or are your allowing your circumstances or feelings to dull your enthusiasm for life and imprison you in a negative frame of mind? You must look through your heart of faith and start seeing yourself as happy, healthy, and whole. That means even when your situation looks bad and on a bleak, when you're tempted to be discouraged or feeling depressed, you must encourage yourself by praying and believing God has something greater than what you had and even though this looks impossible, I know today could be the day that things turn around.

"Today could be the day God restores my marriage. Today could be the day God brings my child home. Today could be the day God takes me from prison to the palace. Today could be the day God restores my business to prosperity. Today could be the day God restores my health. Today could be the day God breaks that generational curse. Today could be the day I get my miracle."

I ask you to keep believing and waiting for these good things to come to fruition in your life. You must make a conscious decision, an act of your will, to maintain an attitude of expectancy and keep your mind filled with thoughts of hope.

Admittedly, sometimes good things don't happen as fast as we would like, but instead of complaining and slouching into negative expectations, we must keep our mind on God. Your attitude should be, "God, I know that you are working in my life"; trials come to test your faith, but stand strong.

I have to share a little story with you, as I journey for the Lord behind prison walls. I lost everything, my home that I the flesh worked so hard to have and Mercedes Benz, but you see, that is a material thing, and God spoke to me behind prison walls and said, "If I blessed you before, what makes you think in your mind that I could not bless you again?" Well. It was painful but the truth, so I started to fast and pray because my God, our God, is about to take me from prison to my palace, only because I believe in him and I have an attitude of expectancy.

Many people sabotage their expectations by negative comments. You know the type:

- "Well, nothing good ever happened to me."
- "I don't think I'll ever bounce back."
- "I owe the federal government a hundred thousand dollars and I may have to file bankruptcy; I'm so swamped with my credit card debt and bills, I can't see any other alternative."
- "I don't see how I could ever be happy again. I've just been through too much pain in my life."

Avoid such negative statements like that; I come to you from experience, and I just got to a point in my life where all I want to do is please and praise God, with an expected end that he will bring me out so that I can continue to tell the world what a mighty God we serve. Low expectations will trap you. You must think positive thoughts. God is a God of abundance and favor.

God brought me out of prison and blessed me where I did not have room enough to receive an overflow, where I did not have to file bankruptcy and all my debt was paid in full.

The Bible says, "If you walk with wise men and women, then you're going to become wise."

If you associate with successful people, before long you will become successful. Their enthusiasm will be contagious, and you will catch that vision. If you stay in an atmosphere of victory, before long you're going to have an image of victory. Once God elevates you to that level, there is no devil in hell that can pluck you out. Expect the favor of God all the time, expect his blessings, and expect to increase. Expect promotion; expect favor on your life. Get up and face tomorrow with enthusiasm, knowing that God has great and big things in store for you. And even when circumstances don't go your way, don't let that get you down. Keep your mind set on God's word.

If you'll do your part by keeping the faith continually contemplating the goodness of Jesus, living with faith and with expectancy, God will take you places you've never even dreamed of; and you'll live at a level you have never before dared to imagine. God has good things in store for you.

If you will change your thinking, God can change your life. God is just; he knows when people aren't treating us right. He knows when we're doing the right thing, yet the wrong thing keeps happening to us. He knows when we're operating with integrity, and yet somebody comes along and cheats us out of what should have been ours. God sees every time you're being taken advantage of. He sees every time you turn the other cheek and let an offense go by. He sees everything you forgive or attempts to restore a broken relationship, even though it wasn't your fault. God sees all that; he's keeping a very good record, and he's promised to take all the evil that comes into your life and turn it around and use it for your good.

Question: Are you willing to change your thinking? Will you take the limits off what God can do in your life? Will you start believing him for bigger and better things? Changes start right here. If you will change your thinking, God can change your life. He doesn't want you to barely get by. He's called El Shaddai, "the God of more than enough."

Good gosh! How much harder can being a Christian be? One answer is found in Matthew 5:48, which says "Be perfect, therefore, as your heavenly Father is perfect." There it is; Jesus tells us one of our goals should be to strive for perfection. None of us walked on water; only our Lord is capable of doing that. Our role is to strive to be like him. Christ commands us to put down our own selfish desires and move toward perfection. To do so requires a real commitment. The Lord needs 100 percent commitment from us. May the world see that we are Christians by our love.

HOLINESS IN SITTING, WALKING, AND TALKING

Having therefore these promises, dearly beloved, let us cleanse ourselves from all filthiness of the flesh and spirit, perfecting holiness in the fear of God. (2 Cor 7:1)

Every new spiritual experience begins with the faith and acceptance of what God has already accomplished for you. God is waiting for you to cease doing! When you have, then he can begin to work in each of our lives.

God's intervention in our lives is truly spontaneous: it happens without any effort on our part. The important thing to remember is not to *try* but rather *trust*, not to demand on man and our own strength but, rather, depend on him.

Nothing is so blessed as when our outward efforts cease, and attitudes become natural and spiritual: when our words, our prayers, our very lives, all become holy. It is then that we experience the unforced expressions of the life of God at work with us.

Too many saints have all the doctrine, but they live lives that contradict that doctrine. God will perfect every man, woman, boy, and girl that has faith in him.

Just as David and his armies fought in spiritual warfare before the rise of the kingdom of Solomon, so it is now. There must first be a period of spiritual warfare, as we saw with David and the works he accomplished with his armies, before the glorious reign of Solomon could begin. God is seeking those who will practice holiness in every aspect of their lives. That means holiness when you are sitting, holiness when you are walking, and holiness when you are talking. He expects it today just as he did from David as he carried out his warfare.

God doesn't just ask us to do the things that are easy for us to do. He asks us to live a life that we believe we can never live and carry out works that we think we can never do.

Many people underestimate the importance of living holy and having a prayer life; they think of it as an emergency measure—something to fall back on when everything else has failed. This is not God's purpose for holiness and prayer; it was never intended to happen that way.

Why does God not declare himself to be the God of Adam? It's because he is the God of the Seed of Faith, not the God of the Seed of the Flesh. That is why God is calling his people to be holy in both their walk and their talk.

The most fundamental sin, according to the Word of God, is disbelief. Lack of belief is the root of all sin. How sad that we pay so little attention to the sin that the Bible emphasizes most.

Today, people tend to look at the fragmentation of sin instead of the root of sin as a whole. By doing so, they disregard the salvation of Christ and pursue human psychological salvation. This offers only moral improvement and a changed lifestyle here on Earth. What's lacking is Life Eternal.

To be baptized means to come out of all the things of the world—to come out and turn away from them! Yet how can we come out of the world? The only way is by dying to the flesh daily. Once the human flesh is dead, the past is finished. Holiness becomes a way of life.

> Follow peace with all men and holiness, without which no man shall see the Lord. (Heb 12:14)

Come out from sin. Why are you so caught up with the world?

> Be ye not unequally yoked together with unbelievers: for what fellowship hath righteousness with unrighteousness? And what communion hath light with darkness?" (2 Cor 6:14)

The Holy Ghost will teach you how to live; just lay aside every sin and watch the Holy Ghost get all over you. The Holy Ghost will keep you from doing wrong. The Holy Ghost will teach you and convict your spirit. The Holy Ghost will guide your steps, your temple, and your attitude. When you become filled with the Holy Ghost, you will find that you are a sweeter person. You will find yourself convinced when you pass a person that you know doesn't like you, and the Holy Ghost causes you to speak anyway. The Holy Ghost will have you watching the company you keep.

Sins of the Spirit are acts such as gossip, envy, pride, and disobedience. Talking too much and telling everything and stubbornness are also sins. God wants his people to be kind to one another by learning to live in peace with all men: black men and Jewish men. When you walk in obedience with the Lord, there is no good thing that God will withhold from you. Everything about you will change. Your life will change; your finances will change. You will never be the same again.

> Follow peace with all men and holiness, without which no man shall see the Lord. (Heb 12:14)

When I get to heaven, I want to see God face-to-face. Let sisterly and brotherly love continue. Be not forgetful to entertain strangers for thereby some have entertained angels unaware. Remember those that are in bonds, as bound with them, and those that suffer adversity, as being yourselves also in the body.

When you wake up in the morning, you can say, "Good morning, Jesus." Jesus was cool.

Holy folks are calm folks; they don't worry about anything. They're peaceful folks; they're prayerful. Holy folks are cool, just like Jesus. Let all seek to be holy because our Heavenly Father is holy.

PRISON LETTERS

June 8, 2006

Dear Corvalis,

Thank you, thank you, thank you . . . you put in words, my life! The Hell turmoil, destructions I was headed into. The shame I couldn't face. You just confirmed what I was just beginning to realize . . . God does not make junk. God does not let us go astray without helping us see the light. Like the poem "footprints" I see . . . you have made me realize that its not too late . . . I can go on now without shame, without heartache because I know God loves me, people like me and everybody-unconditionally!

And thanks to your book . . . I now have renewed strength and greater outlook on my life, my future, My God—Jesus Christ—my Lord and Savoir. You inspire me!!

Thank You,
Love You,
Peace,
Claryce McGee

P.S. I Believe!

Momma C.,

Thank you for your wisdom and kind words. I will always remember you and treasure you. You are a beautiful woman spiritually and physically.

I did my best with my testimony; hopefully, it's good enough and you will use it and appreciate my shortcomings. I've been through more than enough to be 19. I'm very thankful for my experiences and continue to learn from them.

I gave you my word to get back into church, and I will. I will write to you and will always keep in touch.

Continue doing what you do and praising the Lord. You inspire many like myself. I see the joy on your face and know that it's from God. I now want to be filled with the joy that he has for me. I'm ready to grow spiritually and mentally with the Lord.

Thank you for all your comfort and words. You are a golden star in the heavenly skies.

You'll remain in my heart and thoughts.

Your Daughter,
Andrea Patton

I'll miss you and keep me in your prayers!
Thank you again!!

Written by Linda Williams (with a smile)

October 1, 2006

Four years in prison, soon to be five, I already knew four years ago God was doing for me what I didn't want for myself.

After living a life of destruction, all (my life) with different values and qualities in between here and there, and knowing God straight from the first beginning, I still grew up loving the fast life and wanting all that wasn't no good for me.

I experienced four different prison bits starting at the age of thirty-six. I always considered myself of having it made and living good, and that's what kept me coming back and doing what was wrong and liking what *wasn't* no good (for me).

Not until now, between the dates of July 21, 2006, and the time I met Corvalis, I then too realized *again* God was working in my life and was doing for me what I never wanted to do for myself. I grew up with God in my life, thanks to my mother (God rest her soul), so I was able to come to God already knowing what *God is*.

Being butterball naked with all my sins behind me, I'm gaining a new sense of growth and I have my intimacy with God that I truly want to keep!

*Meeting you Corvalis and realizing God was working through you *and* you *not* flaunting or trying to promote your own experiences as a standard *but* rather help me stay focus. I truly appreciate you.*

My End Thoughts

The Fear Factor

The fear of man bringeth a snare: but whoso pulleth his trust in the Lord shall be safe.

Many seek the ruler's favor; but every man's judgment cometh from the Lord. (Prv 29:25,26)

There are many women old and young that come behind prison walls, and their number one reason why the word *fear* enters into their minds is because of what they see on TV in prison.

Behind the prison walls, grandmother, mother, daughter, sister, and family members are afraid of their family member coming out of prison as a bulldagger/lesbian/gay. There are inmates that get hurt physically, and there are inmates that come to prison that simply don't know how to live a healthy and productive life in society. We as people and inmates must take the fear off and live by faith. Fear is abomination to God.

Here is a prime example of one where fear is trying to seep in her life, but the Word of God is rooted down on the inside.

Inmate number 016 phoned home to her husband, and Inmate number 016's husband shared with her news about her son's father: that he didn't want him to bring her son to visit her or simply just spend time with him. Because God's Word is abiding on the inside of Inmate 016,

The Lord is my light and my salvation, whom shall I fear?

The Lord is my strength of my life; of whom shall I be afraid? When the wicked, when my enemies and my foes, come upon me to eat up my flesh, they will stumble and fall. (Ps 27:1-2)

God doesn't want his people to live in fear, but he wants his people to rest in him. "Be still, and know that I am God; I will be exalted among the nation, I will be exalted in the earth" (Ps 46:10).

"When I cried out to God, he heard my cry." Let me explain to you how Inmate 016 felt. Inmate 016 still had some flesh in her that God was trying to get out of her. She cried out to God because she just wanted to visit with her son; she knew that God had already worked out everything while others are trying to figure it out. "I had to rest in God's word."

Living in a fleshly body, you are going to get tired sometimes. Living in a fleshly body, fear is going to arise sometimes. Living in a fleshly body, trials and tribulations are going to happen sometimes.

God did not say how easy it would be, and God did not say how hard it would be either, but he did say that he would never leave us nor forsake us, and he would be with you always. "I can say to you wait on the Lord: be of good courage, and he shall strengthen thine heart; wait I say, on the Lord" (Ps 24:14).

Sometimes, the devil uses the tactics of frustration and fear. It will get you out of vision and will leave you without a purpose.

We need a spirit of restoration. As a believer, you carry the authority.

What will it take for us not to let the devil frustrate you? You got to keep the vision, and the vision is Jesus. God looks at the heart; God sees that you have a mind to live holy. God will help you. Don't be afraid of the devil; call the devil out by his name.

When you are walking in the anointing, you can tell the devil to get out because there is no place for him to grow.

When you stand on holy ground, the devil has no authority over your life.

Don't let the devil frustrate your purpose that God has for your life.

Fear ye not, stand still, and see the salvation of the Lord (Ex 14:13)

The End

Go placidly amid the noise and haste, and remember what peace there may be in silence. As far as possible, without surrender, be on good terms with all persons. Speak your truth quietly and clearly, and listen to others, even the dull and ignorant; they are vexations to the spirit. If you compare yourself with others, you may become vain and bitter; for always, there will be greater and lesser persons than yourself. Enjoy your achievements as well as your plans. Keep interested in your own career, however humble; it is a real possession in the changing fortunes of time. Exercise caution in your business affairs, for the world is full of trickery. But let this not blind you to what virtue there is; many persons strive for high ideas, and everywhere life is full of heroism. Be yourself. Especially, do not feign affection. Neither be cynical about love, for in the face of all aridity and disenchantment, it is perennial as grass. Take kindly that counsel of the years, gracefully surrendering the things of youth. Nurture strength of spirit to shield you in sudden misfortune. But do not distress yourself with imaginings. Many fears are born of fatigue and loneliness. Beyond a wholesome discipline, be gentle with yourself. You are a child of the universe, no less than the trees and the stars; you have the right to be here. And whether or not it is clear to you, no doubt the universe is unfolding as it should. Therefore, be at peace with God, whatever you conceive him to be, and whatever your labors and aspirations, in the noisy confusion of life, keep peace with your soul. With all its sham, drudgery, and shattered dreams, it is still a beautiful world. Be careful. Strive to be happy in God.

Today I'm free to live and not die.
Today I'm free to laugh and not cry.
Today I thank God that I'm free.

PRAYERS

My Prayer

Silence is the only thing that I am able to hear, as I look up to the sky with eyes full of tears. I have so many questions, there are things I don't understand, it's a never ending battle, I need a helping hand.

There are so many roads that go through life, the turns I end up making are the opposite of right. Wrong turns that I make they cut me like a knife, my heart and mind grow weary of all this pain and strife.

My childhood days were bad, but now they are long gone, I never dreamed that bad would come and tag along. Sometimes I feel as though my life is but a curse, right when things get bad it seems they just get worse.

All the songs and things I've read they still ponder in my head, there is a day that I will dread. That day is the day I wake up dead. That's the day I want to miss, so before that happens I must pray this:

Lord I get on my knees and I pray to thee, what is it that I must do to go on with my life and just carry on? He said, "Daughter you must live true." Lord I ask that you forgive me my past and deliver me from temptation. Make my faith strong as I go a long on the path of my destination. Engrave in my heart what keeps me apart from your love and your promise above. Get rid of the sin that lives deep within and keeps me from your gracious hands. Now is my time of need, hear my prayer Lord I plead.

Are there two sets or one print in the sand? It gets harder every day. Satan's always in my way. I can not read or sometimes pray, please just make him go away. Put in me a brand-new heart.

Bless me Lord with a new start. Cleanse my heart mind and soul. Make me spotless like white snow. Help me forgive even myself and not complain when in bad health. To give you praise in good or bad. To wear a smile when sad or mad. To be my strength when I am weak and help me turn the other cheek. With all my tears and heart I pray, what I'm trying so hard to say is to help me live my life so true and help me to be more like you. I feel your touch in all the air as I pray to you my prayer. I know this prayer won't be the last, I'll pray this prayer again, I'll praise you through my time of need. All praise to you!

Amen.

A Prayer for You

Lord Jesus Christ I know how many times you've made a way for me; you've moved my mountains and you've filled my valleys. Lord Jesus do it one more time Lord. Bless every soul behind prison walls here tonight one more time! In the Name of Jesus, Satan, you are a demon of hindrance. I rebuke you, I bind you, and I cast you out in the Name of Jesus. Give your people the victory, Jesus, over all the powers of the enemy. Let all the prisons have a miracle. Let all the prisons have a miracle. Oh God in your name, Jesus, bless everywhere. I know you can work a miracle Jesus. Satan you have to get out of the way; get out of the way you enemy—you demon of darkness—in Jesus's precious name.

The Lord name shall be glorified. In Jesus's name I ask these blessings—walk right when the doors open, walk right in that jail block, walk right in that prison camp, and walk right in that sick body. Praise your way out of that mess—make the misery come out in Jesus's Name by the power of the Holy Ghost, I ask it all. Amen! Amen!

Prayer for Addicted Children

Lord God of Hosts, you are the great Deliverer. We ask you to move mightily on behalf of our children: _____.

Name(s)

Deliver them from evil; show them a way of escape. Convict them of the destructive sin that hurts you so greatly. Father, we are reminding you of your promise—"The seed of the righteous shall be delivered"—and I thank you that the work of the enemy in our children's lives is broken, in Jesus's Name. We are righteous because of the Blood of Jesus, and our children are our seeds. So Lord, deliver them and bring about your good and right and perfect plan for their lives.

Thank you that you know the plans you have for _____ future: plans for their good, not for calamity.

Name(s)

We praise and thank you in advance for the way you will move to save and restore our children because it is not your will that any should perish but that all shall come to repentance. Lord your Word says nothing is impossible for you; I'm standing on that promise! In Jesus's Name, Amen.

Prayer When Our Children Disappoint Us

Lord, I admit there are times when I am so disappointed in my children that I can't see anything good or positive in them.

Forgive me for looking at the imperfections, forgetting that I need to trust you, who does everything in the right way and at the right time. Lord, only you know the deepest needs of my child's heart. Only you know when _____ particular situation is fully ripe for your answer.

Name(s)

Help me to make times of disappointment and heartache times of learning and training for future usefulness. I commit _____ into your hands, Father,

Name(s)

and I thank you that victory is on the way for this child. In Jesus's Name, I pray, with thanksgiving for all your blessings. Amen.

Prayer of Confession and Repentance

Lord Jesus Christ, I acknowledge you as the Son of God, and I thank you for dying on the cross for my sins. You redeemed me from the curse of sin that I might receive your blessings. Father, forgive and cleanse any sin committed by me or my ancestors that exposed our family to a generational curse even to the third, fourth, or tenth generation. I break that generational curse right now over my seed's life. Thank you that my family is freed from *all* past bondages and that you will restore what the enemy has stolen. I love you, Lord. I praise you, Lord. I worship you, Lord. Amen.

"FRIENDS THAT PRAY TOGETHER, STAY TOGETHER"

Dear Lord,

I thank you for this day. I thank you for being able to see and to hear this morning.

I am blessed because you are a forgiving God and an understanding God. You have done so much for me and you keep on blessing me.

Forgive me this day for everything I have done, said, or thought that was not pleasing to you.

I ask now for your forgiveness. Please, keep me safe from all danger and harm.

Help me to start this day with a new attitude and plenty of gratitude.

Let me make the best of each and every day to clear my mind so that I can hear from you.

Please, broaden my mind that I can accept all things.

Let me not whine and whimper over things I have no control over. Let me continue to see sin through God's eyes and acknowledge it as evil.

And when I sin, let me repent and confess with my mouth my wrongdoing and receive the forgiveness of God. And when this world closes in on me, let me remember Jesus's example to slip away and find a quiet place to pray.

It's the best response when I'm pushed beyond my limits.

I know that, when I can't pray, you listen to my heart.

Continue to use me to do your will.

Continue to bless me that I may be a blessing to others.

Keep me strong that I may help the weak.

Keep me uplifted that I may have words of encouragement for others.

I pray for those that are lost and can't find their way.

I pray for the those that are misjudged and misunderstood.

I pray for those that don't pass God's blessings on to others.

I pray for those that don't believe.

I pray for our country and leader.

I pray for those that who are persecuted for Jesus's Name.

I believe that God changed me and that he can change anybody. God changes things.

I pray for all my sisters and brothers.

I pray for each and every family member everywhere.

I pray for peace, love, and joy in their minds, hearts, and homes.

I pray for you to continue to let my flesh die each and every day so that I can see you face-to-face.

I pray that you will receive my tears as sacrifices to you, Lord.

I know that obedience is better than sacrifice.

I pray that every eye that reads this knows there is no problem, circumstance, or situation greater than God. Every battle is in your hands, for you to fight.

I pray these words are received in Jesus's Name.

Amen!

Our Father, who is in Heaven, Hallowed be your Name. Your Kingdom come. Your Will be done on Earth, as it is in Heaven. Our Father, I want to be more reverent in prayer and more unfailing, but the distractions are never ending. Please help me to overcome them. I realize that nothing is hidden from thee and that my heart lies bare and open before thee. Help me to quickly confess my errors, my weakness, and my sin that nothing shall ever stand between me and thee. Anything that I have done, thought, imagined or said that was contrary to thee, I ask thy forgiveness. I thank thee that shame shall not keep me from turning to thee. O God of understanding, guide me, for sometimes, my own words baffle me. Help me not to relate to those around me insensitively. Help me avoid every abuse of speech, and do not allow false and unkind words to escape my lips. I pray that I never speak badly of others or speak empty words of flattery to gain something for myself. Teach me, O Lord, when to keep silent and when to speak; and when I speak, save me from using my words to intentionally humiliate or hurt anyone. Our Father, it is so easy to lash out at the innocent because of my pain. I stand beaten and battered by the countless manifestations of my weakness. O God, it has taken me time, but I am learning to trust thee. When I called, you answered. When I cried, you sent relief. When I was in need, you came through. I know this, but sometimes I forget that you are there for me in every instance. I need only to look, think, and understand; and I can always find you there ready to help me. Thank you, God, for waiting for me to come to thee. *Help me to always live in a state of gratitude. Open my eyes to see the countless and amazing miracles that thou performs for me constantly and that I may still come to thee and present my desires. And because I know thee as the God of all healing, heal me in body and soul. Let all the elements of my body work together in perfect symmetry and in peaceful harmony. Remove from me and all those that I care about every trace of illness, every hint of infirmity; and send healing hidden in the wings of the air we breathe. Help me to understand that life in this world is fleeting, hardly more than a brief breath away. At this moment I am here, as are those around me. Where will I be, where will they be in an hour, in a day, in a year, or in five or ten years? Whatsoever I must do for the good of others, let me do it now, for tomorrow is not promised. Most of all, I pray that the unsaved shall be saved.* And help me to live with joy, overcoming despair, and to seek and find in all things an inkling of thy goodness. Cause me to find deep satisfaction, abiding joy in all that I already have and in all that I do and in all that I am. Protect me with thy love and prevent others from seeing me with hostility to the extent that they wish me harm. Never allow the negativity of others to influence my life or affect my destiny. Teach me patience when I want to run away in the face of challenges or a test. Help me learn to wait for the good that is just around the corner, for the divine help that will soon be within my reach, and for the relief that is jut a moment away. I ask this prayer in the Name of Jesus Christ. Amen. *(If this prayer has been a blessing to you and your family, please write us and let us know).*

Appendix

List of Scriptural Sins To Be Read Before Confessing Your Sins In Prayer

Every yes answer is a sin in your life that needs to be confessed. "Therefore, to one who knows the right thing to do, and does not do it to him it is sin." (Jas 4:17)

1. 1 Thessalonians 5:18 says, "In everything give thanks; for this is God's will for you in Christ Jesus." Do you worry about anything? Have you failed to thank God for all things, the seemingly bad as well as the good? Do you neglect to give thanks at mealtime, openly in front of others?
2. Ephesians 3:20 says, "Now to him who is able to do exceeding abundantly beyond all that we ask or think, according to the power that works within us." Do you fail to attempt things for God because you are not talented enough? Do feelings of inferiority keep you from trying to serve God? When you do accomplish something for Christ, do you fail to give him all the glory?
3. Act 1:8 says, "But you shall receive power when the Holy Spirit has come upon you; and you shall be my witness both in Jerusalem, and in all Judea and Samaria and even to the remotest part of the earth." Have you failed to be a witness with your life for Christ? Have you felt it was enough to just live your Christianity and not witness with your mouth to the lost?
4. Romans 12:3 says, "For . . . I say to every man among you not to think more highly of himself than he ought to think." Are you proud of your accomplishments, your talents, and your family? Do you fail to see others as better than yourself, more important than yourself in the body of Christ? Do you think, as a Christian, you are doing quite well? Do you rebel at God wanting to change you?
5. Ephesians 4:31 says, "Let all bitterness and wrath and anger and clamor and slander be put away from you, along with all malice." Do you complain, find fault, argue? Do you have a critical spirit? Do you carry

a grudge against Christians of another group because they don't see eye to eye with you on all things? Do you speak unkindly about people when they are not present? Are you angry with yourself? Others? God?

6. 1 Peter 2:11 says, "Beloved . . . abstain from fleshly lusts, which wage war against the soul." Are you guilty of lustful eyes toward either sex? Do you fill your mind with pornography or sex-oriented conversation, movies, books? Do you indulge in any lustful activity God's Word condemns—fornication, adultery, perversion?

7. Colossians 3:13 says "Forgiving each other, whoever has a complaint against anyone, just as the Lord forgave you, so also should you." Have you failed to forgive anybody anything that person might have said or done against you? Have you turned certain people off? Are you holding grudges?

WHAT DO THE BEATITUDES MEAN?

Jesus surprised his disciples by telling them what kind of people would be blessed by God. His list of traits are called beatitudes, meaning "to bless" or "to make happy."

Poor of Spirit—This word was taken from a Greek word meaning "to crouch." It can mean lowly, afflicted, helpless, and powerless to solve a problem; lacking wealth and education; or begging. Is there a problem or situation in your life that is beyond your control? Are you reduced to begging God for help? God promises to help the poor of spirit.

Mourn—This word means "to wail." This is deeper than sadness; it is despondency and despair. Do you know anyone who is crushed with disappointments of life? God promises to comfort.

Meek—Meekness means humility, a gentleness of spirit, or a mild disposition. A meek person is one who trust God and accepts today's circumstances as God's best for them, even if situations in their lives are painful, frightening, frustrating, or annoying. Two of the most powerful people in the Bible, Jesus and Moses were considered "meek" (Numbers 12:3).

Hunger and thirst after righteousness—These people eagerly desire (or crave) righteousness. Righteousness is holy and upright living, conforming to God's standard.

Merciful—These people are kind, even to those who treat them without respect. They forgive. God is kind to us, even though sometimes we treat him and his commands without respect. Isaiah 55:7 says, "Let the wicked forsake his way and the evil man his thoughts. Let him turn to the Lord, and he will have mercy on him, and to our God, for he will freely pardon." Is there someone you need to pardon? If we refuse to forgive, God will not forgive us.

Pure of Heart—This person approaches life with innocence and blamelessness. Psalm 73:1 says, "Surely God is good to those who are pure in heart."

Peacemaker—These are people who want peace. They do not stir up fights or arguments. They do not look for reasons to complain or to say bad things about others. James 3:18 says, "Peacemakers who sow in peace, raise a harvest of righteousness."

Persecuted for righteousness—These people are teased, harassed, harmed, or bothered by others because they choose to do what is right. Jesus said, "No servant is greater than his master. If they persecuted me, they will persecute you also." He said, "Rejoice in that day and leap for joy, because great is your reward in heaven" (Lk 6:23). You will have a great reward when you suffer for the Lord.

A Prayer For You And Your Family

PRAYER OF PROTECTION FOR YOUR FAMILY

Father, I thank you for your covenant promise of protection. Right now, I call upon the covenant I have with you and plead the Blood of Jesus over my family, husband, wife, my children, and myself, God.

Angels, I charge you to watch over my family to protect us, for we are walking in the footsteps of Jesus. Go before us, behind us, beside us, and all the way around us. Keep us from calamity, evil, and misfortune (Name all names to the Lord).

No evil will befall my family in the Name of Jesus! No weapon formed against them will prosper, and every lying tongue that rises up against them I do condemn, for this is my heritage as a servant of the Lord. I thank you, Father, that great is the peace of my children.

Their righteousness is of you. They don't walk in their own righteousness, but in your righteousness by the Blood of Jesus.

I thank you for that, Lord. They will not get off track in life, none of their steps shall slide (Psalm 37:31) for your Holy Spirit will guide them every step of the way.

Father, your word says that we your sheep know your voice. It says you will show us things to come. It says the voice of your spirit will come to us and say, "This is the way; walk in it." I stand on these promises, Lord, and ask that you teach us to hear your voice.

Help us recognize when you are speaking to us, and we will obey. Now I stand in your Holy of Holies and open my spirit to receive the wisdom you have afforded me. I put myself in a position to hear and receive instruction from you. I enter the secret place of the Most High by the Blood of the Lamb, and I purpose to live my life in your presence.

I thank you that you are faithful to your word, Father. I thank you that what you say is certain and sure. When you say you will deliver us, we can rely on that promise. So right now I receive your supernatural protection and deliverance for my family and me.

In Jesus's Name! Amen

Psalm 23

The Lord is my shepherd; I shall not want he makes me to lie down in green
    pastures;
He leads me beside still waters. He restores my soul;
He leads me in the paths of righteousness for his name's sake.
Yea, though I walk through the valley of the shadow of death,
I will fear no evil; For you art with me;
Thy rod and staff will comfort me.
Thou prepare a table before me in the presence of mine enemies;
Thou anoint my head with oil; my cup runneth over surely goodness and mercy
shall follow me all the days of my life;
And I will dwell in the house of the Lord
Forever amen.

ORDER FORM

JSI Incorporated
5900 Glen Rock Ave. Suite 101
Fort Washington, MD 20744
301-536-7163—Office

Please send me *Behind Prison Walls: Inmate Number 27773-016*
Jehovah Sermonette: Empowering Uplifting Daily Bread
Rising Above Your Struggles: Life Transforming Truth
Touched by an Angel: A Spiritual Motivational Book

Quantity:

Price:

Name:
Company:
Address:
City State:
Zip code:

Home Phone:
Work Phone:
Fax Number:
E-mail:

Shipping:

Method of Payment: Check _____ Cash _____

Driver's License No. with all check orders: